ENDING GENERATIONAL POVERTY

(Learning to Love Your Neighbor)

by

Keith Rodriguez
Nelson Warner

Copyright © 2021
by
Keith Rodriguez
Nelson Warner
All Rights Reserved

No part of this book may be reproduced or transmitted in any form or by any means, electronic or mechanical, including photocopying, recording, or by an information storage and retrieval system, without permission in writing from the authors.

ISBN:

First Printing: 2021

The "K2" Series of books quotes and identifies the following versions of scripture: Scripture quotations taken from the Amplified® Bible (AMP), Copyright © 2015 by The Lockman Foundation Used by permission. Scripture quotations taken from the Amplified® Bible (AMPC), Copyright © 1954, 1958, 1962, 1964, 1965, 1987 by The Lockman Foundation Used by permission. Scripture taken from the Common English Bible®, CEB® Copyright © 2010, 2011 by Common English Bible.™ Used by permission. All rights reserved worldwide. Scripture quotations marked (CEV) are from the Contemporary English Version Copyright © 1991, 1992, 1995 by American Bible Society, Used by Permission. Complete Jewish Bible (CJB), Copyright © 1998 by David H. Stern. All rights reserved. No portion of this book may be reproduced, stored in a retrieval system, or transmitted in any form or by any means without prior written permission of the publisher. Scripture quotations marked (ERV) are taken from Easy-to-Read Version, Copyright © 2006 by Bible League international Scripture quotations are from The ESV® Bible (The Holy Bible, English Standard Version®), copyright © 2001 by Crossway, a publishing ministry of Good News Publishers. Used by permission. All rights reserved. Scripture taken from The Expanded Bible (EXB). Copyright ©2011 by Thomas Nelson. Used by permission. All rights reserved.

Scripture quotations marked (GNT or TEV; Formerly Today's English Version, TEV) are from the Good News Translation in Today's English Version- Second Edition Copyright © 1992 by American Bible Society. Used by Permission. Scripture is taken from GOD'S WORD®, © 1995 God's Word to the Nations. Used by permission of Baker Publishing Group. Scripture quotations marked (ISV) are taken from the Holy Bible: International Standard Version®. Copyright © 1996-forever by The ISV Foundation. ALL RIGHTS RESERVED INTERNATIONALLY. Used by permission. Scripture quotations marked (KJV) are taken from the King James Version that is in public domain. Scripture quotations marked (MSG) are taken from THE MESSAGE. Copyright © by Eugene H. Peterson 1993, 1994, 1995, 1996, 2000, 2001, 2002. Used by permission of NavPress. All rights reserved. Represented by Tyndale House Publishers, Inc. Scripture texts, prefaces, introductions, footnotes and cross references used in this work are taken from the New American Bible (NABRE), revised edition © 2010, 1991, 1986, 1970 Confraternity of Christian Doctrine, Inc., Washington, DC All Rights Reserved. No part of this work may be reproduced or transmitted in any form or by any means, electronic or mechanical, including photocopying, recording, or by any information storage and retrieval system, without permission in writing from the copyright owner. Scripture quotations taken from the New American Standard Bible® (NASB), Copyright © 1960, 1962, 1963, 1968, 1971, 1972, 1973,1975, 1977, 1995 by The Lockman Foundation Used by permission. Scripture quotations marked (NIV) are taken from THE HOLY BIBLE, NEW INTERNATIONAL VERSION®, NIV® Copyright © 1973, 1978, 1984, 2011 by Biblica, Inc.® Used by permission. All rights reserved worldwide. Scripture quotations marked (NKJV) are taken from the New King James Version®. Copyright © 1982 by Thomas Nelson, Inc. Used by permission. All rights reserved. Scripture quotations marked (NLT) are taken from the Holy Bible, New Living Translation, copyright © 1996, 2004, 2007, 2015 by Tyndale House Foundation. Used by permission of Tyndale House Publishers, Inc., Carol Stream, Illinois 60188. Copyright Information © Christian Literature International (CLI) is a non-profit ministry dedicated to publishing and providing the Word of God in a form that can be read and understood by new readers and the well-educated alike. . . and at an affordable price. We invite you to learn how the NEW LIFE Version unlocks the treasures of God's Word! All rights reserved. Scripture quotations marked (OJB) are taken from The Orthodox Jewish Bible fourth edition, OJB. Copyright 2002, 2003, 2008, 2010, 2011 by Artists for Israel International. All rights reserved. Scripture quotations marked (PHILLIPS) are taken from J. B. Phillips, "The New Testament in Modern English", 1962 edition, published by HarperCollins. Scripture quotations marked (TLB) are taken from The Living Bible copyright © 1971. Used by permission of Tyndale House Publishers, Inc., Carol Stream, Illinois 60188. All rights reserved. Scripture taken from The Voice™. Copyright © 2008 by Ecclesia Bible Society. Used by permission. All rights reserved. Scripture quotations marked (WEB) are taken from World English Bible which is in public domain. Scripture quotations marked (WNT) are taken from Weymouth New Testament) 1903 which is in public domain. Scripture quotations marked (YLT) are taken from Young's Literal Translation which is in public domain.

CONTENTS

ACKNOWLEDGEMENTS	vii
FOREWARD	viii
ABOUT THE COVER	xi
INTRODUCTION	xiii
GOD-GIVEN HUMAN DIGNITY	1
Why Human Dignity Matters	1
The Theology of Dignity and the Fall of Man	3
Poverty, Race, and Human Dignity	6
POVERTY	12
Introduction: Poverty and the Dignity of Man	12
What is Poverty?	13
The Poor in Scripture	13
Features of Poverty	15
Finding the Causes of Poverty	17
Poverty of the Mind, Heart, and Body	18
The Root Cause of Poverty	19
Idolatry	22
Christians and Poverty Alleviation	25
How Do Christians Misunderstand Poverty?	27
So, Why Is Jesus So Concerned About Poverty?	29
LOVE	33
Agape Love	36
The Two Sides of the Love Coin	42
Work and Love	47

WHOLE PEOPLE, WHOLE COMMUNITY	**50**
The Beloved Whole Community	50
The Broken Community	54
The Incarnational Community	57
Becoming Whole People	61
Justice and the Whole Community	64
What Causes Injustice?	66
The Two Sides of Justice	69
Why Are So Many Christians Blind to the Empowerment Gap?	72
The Vision of Shalom	73
Strengthening Social Capital	75
NEXT STEPS	**80**
Establishing a Vision	82
Common Groan	84
So, How Is This to Be Done?	85
Learning to Love	86
Three R's of Christian Development	87
Our Three Major Delivery Systems	89
Conclusion	104

ACKNOWLEDGEMENTS

There are several people to thank without whose assistance this book would not have been completed. John Perkins of the Perkins Foundation and godfather of the Christian Community Development Association and Jimmie Dorrell of Mission Waco, another community development guru, whose mentorship, direction and support have helped create the vision for this book. Bridge Ministry of Acadiana and the children and adults in the neighborhood Bridge serves who provided the inspiration. Dr. William B. Allen, Chief Operating Officer for the Center for Urban Renewal and Education (CURE) for his encouragement and wonderfully edifying comments upon first reviewing our initial manuscript. And he provided the Foreword for the book. Mikael Rose Good (CURE) who took our raw manuscript and provided her "magic" editing skills to enhance the final document. Jules Edwards and Pat Trahan who worked with us a decade ago on the concepts of our three major delivery systems and a general plan. Ray Ogle, whose technical computer skills made this final product a reality. Finally, to our wives Jan (Nelson) and Janet (Keith) who willingly and graciously gave us the space, time and encouragement for this book.

FOREWARD

"Vine and fig for all" expresses the realistic expectation of the biblical injunction to all humankind: "everyone under his/her own vine and fig tree." That is not a utopian, socialistic dream. It is instead the rendering of a moral understanding of what living rightly means.

Nothing is more important than to free ourselves from the totalitarian nightmare of enforced conformity in the name of material prosperity in order to embrace the humanizing influence of a belief that all may benefit from faithful submission to divine order. That is the vein in which the prophet responds to the inquiry, "what does God ask of you," with the comprehensive injunction "to do justly, and to love mercy, and to walk humbly with your God." The very iterative form of the expression illustrates that it designates a succession of conduct-governing prescriptions with practical effect. "Doing justly" means precisely undertaking in particular cases to do what is right. It is not, in short, attitudinal. It is rather a moral injunction to do and not merely to believe. Similarly, to love mercy indicates a disposition to undertake acts of mercy—for love expresses being drawn to the particular need. And, finally, "to walk humbly with your God" conveys moving through life with a determination to follow the will of God in preference to one's own will.

This is the formula that *Ending Generational Poverty* has derived from an attentive regard for the word of God as applied to the necessities of the world in which we live. The conclusion that believers have much to contribute toward responding to the present necessities—nay, more, can decisively respond to the present necessities—amounts to a practical guide for recovery in the face of what often seem to be intractable dilemmas (or "groans" as the authors so aptly describe them).

When confronted with the question, what do we have to contribute to the apparently overwhelming sufferings of under-resourced children in distressed communities, they begin by rejecting the self-excusing interpretation that the problems are overwhelming. They point out that "with God all things are possible." It becomes, therefore, an index of moral purpose and religious belief that one rejects the despairing sense of being overwhelmed. Further, it evinces strong confidence in the potential of human beings to attain to the proficiency conveyed in the vision of "everyone under his/her own vine and fig tree." This positive, hopeful vision empowers as well as commands people committed to justice and mercy to begin to move in the world and to refuse to substitute hand-wringing for doing, acting, and submitting humbly to the task before us.

The authors have done what CURE urges us all to do—namely, to identity the opportunity "to go and do" in order to fulfill the obligation to which we are subject. They begin by embracing the call to "relocate" where the need is and there to bring the power of fellowship to the work of development. Interpreted, this means not treating people in need as subjects or patients but rather as brothers and sisters in whose interests one finds one's own interest. Only then does the offer and provision of resources and training gain meaningful traction. What this means for individuals, churches, businesses, and governments is that there is no place for remote charity that can make a difference. True generosity recognizes no Samaritans; all are our fellows.

    W. B. Allen
    Chief Operating Officer
    Center for Urban Renewal and Education

ABOUT THE COVER

(a visual representation of the absence of poverty)

WHOLENESS. (Whole Kingdom People, Neighborhood & Community) The circle represents a vision of wholeness, as in the Kingdom of God on earth as it is in heaven.

Bridge Ministry of Acadiana (BMA) simply defines a whole person as being both 'capable' and 'caring - developed hearts and minds. Whole people make up whole marriages. Whole marriages make up whole families, and whole families make up whole neighborhoods and a whole commUNITY. All is one in unity in Christ. The Hebrews use the term "Shalom", meaning wholeness, peace and joy. This is the good soil (Luke 8:15) of discipleship.

BRIDGE(s) OF RECONCILIATION & FRIENDSHIP. Thus, as Ambassadors of Reconciliation, we are called to bridge our relational gaps and become friends with God and each other. These relational bridges connect and facilitate resource flow and trade that build whole people both mentally (mind) & spiritually (heart). God's bridges of reconciliation intentionally end in friendships and are for the betterment of all. That is, God's bridges are designed for two-way traffic where resources flow between both sides and neither side becomes depleted, but built up. These bridges are intentionally built with truth and love. God's truth promises to set us free (John 8:32). This is a love that does not create dependency and harm, but a love that builds up (1 Cor 8:1), develops, and empowers a person to be both a capable and caring member of the human family .... and this agape love promises to never fail (1 Cor 13:8).

THE CROSS OF JESUS CHRIST. None of this is remotely possible without the Cross of Jesus Christ whose Spirit and Word now lives in us who love Him. The Cross is created by our loving relationships vertically with God and horizontally with mankind: (Matthew 22:37-40) to love God, others and self wholeheartedly. The cross and carrying our cross daily (Luke 9:23) is where our meaning, purpose and true identity is found in Christ Jesus.

The Vision (the Goal) is 'Character' ... The Character of Christ.
The Mission (the Path to the Goal) is 'Love' ... Agape Love.

INTRODUCTION

In 2002, an anonymous donation of $150,000 was made to our church, Trinity Bible Church in Lafayette, LA, with only one string attached: we must use the money to build an inner-city ministry that goes beyond "feeding fish" to the hungry. Our church had a missional bent, regularly serving in various places overseas. But with this donation, instead of crossing the ocean, many church members now only had to cross the railroad tracks to participate in mission work.

It took a year of study, research, guidance, and prayer for us to decide what God wanted the church to do. We received guidance primarily from Jimmy Dorrell, the pastor of the Church Under the Bridge in Waco, Texas (www.churchunderthebridge.org) and the co-founder of Mission Waco (www.missionwaco.org/mission-waco), who offered us a biblical model for the kind of inner-city development program God wanted us to implement. Jimmy became our coach. He taught us the theology of inner-city mission and how to make our faith relevant in the lives of inner-city residents. He taught us a practical faith that begins and ends in love.

In 2002, Jimmy directed us to the Christian Community Development Association (www.CCDA.org). He recommended practical books of faith to read and study. He guided us in acquiring the right biblical principles of development before we began our ministry. Beginning with the right principles and making sure we value what God values has proven critical to our ministry's success. With God at the helm and in bold faith, we created the Bridge Ministry of Acadiana and moved into an inner-city neighborhood, just as Jesus moved into our neighborhood.

Small wood-frame houses, some little more than shacks; dead-end streets without sidewalks; railroad tracks running through the middle of the neighborhood; very few actual homeowners. This is the reality of an inner-city Lafayette neighborhood populated by our under-resourced neighbors. Oh, and don't forget the occasional shooting. Some people work, but most are on government assistance (just as their mothers were), and even those with jobs are on Medicaid. Some people are illiterate, or read at no higher than a third or fifth-grade level.

In 2003, Bridge Ministry (Bridge) rented a house in one of these under-resourced neighborhoods where drug trafficking, prostitution, and crime were most visible. We began going door to door to learn about our neighbor's dreams. People told us they dreamed of having safe streets and secure homes again. They dreamed of a neighborhood free of drugs and prostitution. They also dreamed of having respectful children who did well in school and beyond. They were not dreaming of more "relief" from charitable outsiders, but of "development and empowerment." Using their hopes and dreams of development as a guide, we began building multifaceted, relational, daily programs that the neighborhood and its children readily embraced.

The Bridge eventually became a member of the Christian Community Development Association (CCDA), where 3,000-plus faithful urban missionaries come together every year from around the United States (and beyond) to share in a variety of practical inner-city workshops (faith-shops), fellowship, and worship. The CCDA was founded by John M. Perkins of Jackson, Mississippi. Along with Dr. Dorrell and Dr. Perkins, we have been blessed by many other CCDA mentors, including Dr. Wayne Gordon, Glen Kehrein (deceased), Dr. Soong-Chan Rah, Dr. Amy Sherman, Mo Leverett, Lowell Noble, Mary Nelson, and Dr. Robert Lupton. By sitting at Jesus' feet and theirs, we are learning how to make our faith relevant and how to wholeheartedly love God, self, and our neighbors in right and meaningful ways for the sake of God's kingdom and glory.

Once the Bridge was up and running, our main focus, as directed by the neighborhood, was the children. We began offering after-school tutoring and homework assistance (for which we enlisted the aid of dozens of volunteers from several churches) along with regular children's Bible studies. To that, we added adult Bible studies, clubs, gatherings for potluck meals, summer day camps, a neighborhood committee that meets with city officials and the police department to air its concerns, and more.

One of our adult programs for the past sixteen years has been a weekly Bible study for the men of the neighborhood, with a few men outside the neighborhood attending too. The men range in age from early forties to late eighties. Over time, the leadership of the study has been taken over by four of our neighbors. Each week, someone volunteers to prepare a meal for about twenty people ("Best $2 meal in town!"). We do not sing hymns, but everything else about this gathering is church—discussing God's Word, "breaking bread" together, and sharing life as friends. Most of these men have known each other for most of their lives. The older men reminisce about neighborly relationships and whole families that were the norm fifty years ago. They speak to the fact that since the 1970s, trusting relationships have steadily fallen within the neighborhood, while crime has gone up. They reflect on a neighborhood that has become more and more disconnected, both within and with respect to the larger community. Since 2000, about 66% of the neighborhood's homes have become owned by outsiders, with renters only staying three to four years on average. "We Buy Homes" signs are plastered on every telephone pole.

After a few years of ministry, we realized we needed to expand our capacity. Our 1500-square-foot house was just too small to hold fifty to sixty kids each day. Once we turned the issue over to the Holy Spirit, miracles began to occur. We found two acres available a couple of blocks from our rent house fronting on one of Lafayette's main streets. A friend donated $170,000 to buy the land. After a year, we had raised about half a million dollars in our building fund, but we knew this would not be enough. Out of the blue, the city's Community Development Department gave us $450,000—with no strings attached! We were able to build two 2500-square-foot classroom buildings with no debt.

After several more years, we realized that two and half hours in the afternoon was not enough time with these kids. Many of the kids in third grade and above were one to two years behind. We knew we could do better. So, in 2016, we went to work on a plan to open our own school. With fits and starts we got through two years, but it became clear that our school needed a real leader—a person with administrative experience in a Christian school. Time for another miracle.

Vanessa Bell, previously a teacher and administrator at a Christian school in Lafayette, had retired a few years ago and moved to Colorado with her new husband. Because her mother was ill, she regularly travelled to Lafayette to care for her. It was during one of these trips that we were put in touch with Vanessa to discuss the possibility of her taking over as principal. Her first question told us all we needed to know: "Do you want a Christian school or a Christ-centered school? There's a difference, you know!" We knew instantly that God had brought the right person to us. And after a couple weeks of prayer, Vanessa knew that God had brought her to the right place. To give you an idea of Vanessa's heart, take a look at an excerpt from her first Bridge Community Christian School newsletter:

"Many children of Bridge Community Christian School live with a distant view of first world privileges, ideals and thoughts. More than a few of the Bridge children exist within the reality of a "third world" environment. How can this be remotely possible, in a country so rich? Simply put, it's possible when you live in the most under-resourced forgotten part of town. People drive past our neighborhood, but don't stop by because the thought is there's NOTHING there for me or anyone I know or care about or surely, it's too dangerous to live in "that part of town." I've talked with many of the children about their dreams and hopes for a better life and future. Most have no road map and in many cases no frame of reference. I have also witnessed encouraging moments of JOY as a child learns, maybe for the first time, that many in authority desire to protect and not harm them. There's hope that people really care about who they are and are delighted to help them on their journey to what they want to become. I've seen children's eyes light up as they experience something NEW, as simple as a canvas art project or a different style of music. I've witnessed first-hand what happens when children experience people that believe the BEST of them and give the BEST to them.

Bridge Community Christian School educates, nurtures and empowers low income students to impact the world. We offer an excellent Christ Centered education. Our small class sizes equip teachers to personally interact and academically invest with each student and parent. We're intentional about creating a Christ Centered Culture that fosters and promotes a safe environment to learn and grow in. We want to create opportunities for a vast pool of career choices and introduce the children to new experiences and adventures, all while developing a Biblical World View."

Throughout the years, Bridge has struggled with the question of how to love our inner-city neighbors. Ultimately, we have learned to love our neighbors mainly by loving their children. We have witnessed generational poverty and its effects firsthand since 2003, and we have come to realize the importance of breaking the cycle.

At one point during our ministry, four of our board members decided to delve deeper into generational poverty (which is defined as poverty that persists for at least two generations, whereas situational poverty is defined as a lack of resources due to a particular event such as death, divorce, or illness). They came up with a possible solution—the one that is further developed in this book. The basis of their solution was the blend of grace, love, and truth that is held to be crucial by most followers of Jesus. Unfortunately, the economic meltdown of 2008/09 intervened in their work, and the focus moved elsewhere.

Recently, however, we saw the most glaring evidence yet of the destructive nature of generational poverty. Our school is free for those who earn less than twice the poverty rate. The only requirement is that parents apply in a timely manner to the state for a scholarship. The process is fairly simple, but time-sensitive.

When we saw that many of the parents did not even want to take the necessary steps to get their child a quality Christian education, letting them remain in a D or F school instead, we realized how deeply generational poverty had penetrated their lives. We came to realize that the crux of the problem was the damage done to their God-given dignity. At creation, God declared that man would be made in His own image and likeness. With that came a dignity that is foundational to our significance and our happiness as human beings. But with the Fall, our inherent dignity was tarnished by sin.

Our eighteen years of experience have taught us that the causes of generational poverty run much deeper than conventional thought perceives. Generational poverty is multifaceted and must be attacked in a multifaceted manner. Overcoming it is not going to be cheap, quick, or without pain. But in our struggles, we who choose to love God and our neighbor will grow and mature into Christlike character. And in seeking to restore our neighbors' dignity and bring them to a place of shalom (i.e., wholeness, peace and joy), we will find shalom too, both individually and collectively.

CHAPTER ONE

GOD-GIVEN HUMAN DIGNITY

Why Human Dignity Matters

According to Scripture, every man, woman, and child is created in the image of God. This truth is the foundation of our ministry and the premise of the argument laid out in this book. In the first chapter of the book of Genesis, God says, "Let us make man in our image, in our likeness" (Gen. 1:26). This means that every person you will ever encounter bears the image of God—the imago Dei—on their soul. Because we are made in the image of God, we are each born with an innate dignity. Webster's defines dignity as "the state or quality of being excellent, worthy or honorable." That is, *every* person is excellent, worthy, and honorable. This is our spiritual identity, and if we believe it, our belief manifests itself in various forms of behavior. Unfortunately, often we do not recognize our own dignity or that of others. We typically pick and choose who we think exhibits dignified qualities in speech and behavior. But the dignity that comes from the Creator's image is not dependent on man's behavior.

Then why, we might ask, does there often seem to be a gap between man's innate dignity and his behavior? After creation came man's Fall from God's glory. Mankind now lives in an identity crisis. The imago Dei is tarnished, marred, and sometimes unrecognizable due to sin. But we have not lost our dignity. Sin does not eradicate the fact that "God made human beings in his own image" (Gen. 9:5–6). This knowledge—that we are created in the image of God—is essential to have if we are to live as God designed us to live. We should be filled with compassion for those who are unenlightened to this truth. Without knowledge of his dignity, the individual loses nearly all hope.

The depth of mankind's problem is excellently characterized by Laura Hillenbrand in her biography of Louis Zamperini, entitled *Unbroken*. Zamperini was an Olympic runner who participated in the Berlin Olympics. In World War II, his plane crashed in the Pacific. He was ultimately rescued, but ended up in Japanese prisoner-of war-camps where he was severely mistreated. Hillenbrand writes:

"The crash of the *Green Hornet* had left Louie and Phil in the most desperate physical extremity, without food, water, or shelter. But on Kwajalein, the guards sought to deprive them of something that had sustained them even as all else had been lost: dignity. This self-respect and sense of self-worth, the innermost armament of the soul, lies at the heart of humanness; to be deprived of it is to be dehumanized, to be cleaved from, and cast below mankind. Men subjected to dehumanizing treatment experience profound wretchedness and loneliness and find that hope is almost impossible to retain. Without dignity, identity is erased.... Dignity is as essential to human life as water, food, and oxygen."[1]

Our God-given dignity is essential to our humanity, and a mutual recognition of dignity is the most important component of our identity and all human relationships.

The Theology of Dignity and the Fall of Man

God has a worth and a value higher than any of us can imagine. Since we are created in His image, we have immense value as well. At His creation, as part of the imago Dei, man was given dominion over the land and every living creature (Gen. 1:28), but this purpose was partially hampered by the Fall. The writer of Hebrews tells us the same thing: after quoting Psalm 8, which describes just how incredible man is in God's eyes, he goes on to say that although all things were made subject to man, that position was lost.

" 'What is mankind that you are mindful of them, a son of man that you care for him? You made them a little lower than the angels; you crowned them with glory and honor and put everything under their feet.'

In putting everything under them, God left nothing that is not subject to them. Yet at present we do not see everything subject to them." (Heb. 2:6–8, NIV).

The study notes in the NASB Study Bible for v. 8 state, "God's purpose from the beginning was that man should be sovereign in the creaturely realm subject only to God. Due to sin

---

[1] Laura Hillenbrand, Unbroken: A World War II Story of Survival, Resilience, and Redemption (New York: Random House, 2014), 188–89.

that purpose of God has not yet been fully realized." Even though Jesus' sacrifice put to death the "old man," that is, the sin nature inherited from our original parents, the "flesh" is something Christ followers still have to deal with as they go through the sanctification process.

No matter how one looks at the story of Adam and Eve—historical event, allegory, or anything in between—the truth is that every member of the human race, when given free will to choose, will sooner or later choose themselves over God.

Watchman Nee, in his classic work *The Normal Christian Life,* describes this very well. The passage is worth quoting at length:

"Adam was created a living soul, with a spirit inside to commune with God and with a body outside to have contact with the material world....

Adam was created perfect—by which we mean that he was without imperfections because created by God—but that he was not yet perfected. He needed a finishing touch somewhere....

God was seeking to have not merely a race of men of one blood upon the earth, but a race which had, in addition, His life resident within its members. Such a race will eventually compass Satan's downfall and bring to fulfillment all that God has set his heart upon. It is this that was in view with the creation of man....

God's goal in man was "sonship," or in other words, the expression of His life in human sons. That divine life was represented in the garden, as we saw, by the tree of life, bearing a fruit that could be accepted, received, taken in.

If Adam, created neutral, were voluntarily to turn that way and, choosing dependence upon God, were to receive of the tree of life (representing God's own life), God would then have that life in union with men; He would have secured His spiritual sons. But if instead Adam should turn to the tree of the knowledge of good and evil, he would as a result be "free," in the sense of being able to develop himself on his own lines apart from God....

Standing between two trees, he yielded to Satan."[2]

Unfortunately, Adam chose to eat from the tree of knowledge of good and evil, thus choosing to rely on his own soul (mind and will) and to depend on self instead of God. In truth, this choice against God was a decision for Satan. And since we are all descendants of Adam, we are each agents of Satan as well. Remember, God warned Adam and Eve that they would die if they ate from this tree. He was referring to spiritual death—separation from God. The characteristics of this spiritual death, which are passed down through Adam's race, are what we call "sin nature." At its root, sin nature is defined by choosing to love self over God. That choice is the root cause of the sins we commit. The result is that the inherent dignity with which we were each created is no longer bright and shiny, visible to everyone, but becomes tarnished—just like silver that never gets polished.

But Jesus, our Savior and Redeemer, is the restorer of our dignity through His Word and Spirit. As Paul writes in Romans 7:24–25, "What a wretched man I am! Who will rescue me from this body that is subject to death? Thanks be to God, who delivers me through Jesus Christ our Lord!" We are all, therefore, in Christ: in His death on the cross (Rom. 6:3) and in His resurrection (Rom. 6:5, 8) set free from condemnation (Rom. 8:1), made a new creation reconciled to God (2 Cor. 5:17, 18), and destined to

---

[2] Watchman Nee, *The Normal Christian Life* (Wheaton, IL: Tyndale House Publishers, 1977), 224–26.

become the wisdom of God who is our righteousness, holiness, and redemption (1 Cor. 1:30).

This is our new and true nature and identity in Christ. The Holy Spirit now dwells in us and leads us to look (i.e., act, think, and talk) like Jesus (Rom. 8:29). As God works in us, we take on His very character, and our dignity begins to be restored to its former visible splendor.

Poverty, Race, and Human Dignity

But the restoration of dignity is not so easily retained for many people. It is a daily struggle to carry our cross. Particularly relevant to this work are the poor, who have less of a foundation to stand on to embrace their God-given dignity. When a person's life becomes emptied of meaning and appears hopeless, his sense of dignity is diminished or even crushed. To demonstrate this, we should examine how poverty and the diminishment of dignity have worked together in our own country's history.

While it may sound trite, it is nonetheless true that in America, many of the problems of poverty find their roots in slavery. While this book is about generational poverty, we must address the fact that poverty has continued to disproportionately afflict African-Americans in our country. Without going into a detailed history, until the end of the Civil War in America, the culture and all the basic institutions of society worked together to justify and enable the dehumanization of African-Americans through slavery. Chief among the reasons for this was economic self-interest—a characteristic which still commands a high place in many areas of society, as do so many other "false gods" like success, materialism, power, sex, and "religion." Even after slavery ended, cultural and social institutions were so deeply inbred with attitudes of discrimination and inequality that the plight of black men and women appeared to be hardly changed. John Perkins, in his book *A Quiet Revolution*, captures the desperation of this situation quite well:

"Imagine that you are one of the first persons to be told after more than 200 years of captivity and dependence that you are now "free." You can't read or write. You have come to know marriage as that transitory interchange between a black man and a black woman that produces children and lasts as long as "death or distance do them part." You have experienced how black men are "bred" with black women, how children are later separated from their "families." You have no money, no stable religion, no silverware, no towels, and no bed sheets. Chances are your primary skill is manual farm labor. You have no land.

But, you are free. And where does that leave you? The same place you were before "freedom": total dependence. That's what the slave system created in black people. So deep is the dependence that former slaves not only relied on their white masters for their economic well-being, but also for their culture, their religion, their affirmation...even their names."[3]

God released the Israelites from the oppression of Egyptian slavery and empowered them with Egyptian gold and silver and the Promised Land (Exodus 3:8, 22). In the New Covenant, Christ came to lovingly free us from the oppression of sin and empower believers with the indwelling Holy Spirit and His Word. In both

---

[3] John Perkins, *A Quiet Revolution* (Pasadena, CA: Urban Family Pubications, 1976), 91.

cases, God does not merely take away the power that enslaves His people—He gives them new power to grow in Him. We learn from this that no long-term oppression can ever be solved by "release" alone. Release alone often morphs into a subtler oppression, as when the emancipation of slaves in America morphed into Jim Crow segregation, which after the Civil Rights era morphed into entitlements. For full justice to be done, release must always be followed by development and empowerment. This is true for alcoholics, drug addicts (or any type of addict), sex offenders, or anyone with a history of spending a good deal of time in jail. Without some form of changed behavior effected through development and empowerment, they have virtually no chance of righting their lives. This is especially true of America's "freed" slaves. The absence of empowerment results in total dependence and a lack of ability to do for oneself. Perkins continues, "But we discovered that as black people we cannot act in our own best interest. That is perhaps the saddest thing about a people who have been historically or long-term oppressed. C. S. Lewis described it when he said, "One of the worst results of being a slave is that when there is no one to force you any more you find you have lost the power of forcing yourself." [4]

Poverty by its very nature requires all thought to be directed toward the problem of surviving today, leaving no time to think about the future. There can be no hopes, no dreams, no imagining what could be. This was the condition of many blacks even after they were freed from slavery. As time went on, many blacks moved north to seek factory jobs that sprang up during and after World War II. But even in northern cities, false gods led to the

---

[4] Perkins, *A Quiet Revolution*, 92.

oppression of blacks, making it difficult for them to attain higher levels of success. By the time of the Civil Rights Act, blacks were seriously in need of a helping hand—something that would level the playing field, enabling them to obtain a place in society and empowering them to realize the "American Dream." But government assistance given to an already dependent people will just create deeper dependence—and this is exactly where we find ourselves decades later. All relevant statistics from slavery to Jim Crow to entitlements bear this out.

Dean Kalahar quotes research by Thomas Sowell that demonstrates the point.[5] In 1950, 72% of all black men and 81% of black women had been married. Every census from 1890 to 1950 showed that black labor force participation exceeded whites. Prior to the 1960s, the unemployment rate for black sixteen- and seventeen-year-olds was under 10%. In 1965, 76.5% of black children were born to married women. Since the 1960s, however, black labor force participation rates have been lower than that of whites, and unemployment rates for black sixteen- and seventeen-year-olds have never dropped below 20%. In 1980, 31% of all black first-born children were born to teenage mothers. By 1992, 54% of all black children were living only with their mothers. In the 1980s and 90s, an absolute majority of black families with no husband lived in poverty. In addition to the statistics noted above, it is common knowledge that illegitimacy rates in the black community are very high. High school graduation rates are low,

---

[5] Dean Kalahar, "The Decline of the African-American Family," *American Thinker*, March 29, 2014, www.americanthinker.com/articles/2014/03/the_decline_of_the_africanamerican_family.html.

and unemployment rates are higher than the average for all Americans. Teen unemployment is over 40%.[6] This has been reality for a large portion of the black community for generations.

While discrimination in a lot of areas has been reduced and eliminated under the Civil Rights Act, the destruction of the black family has grown far worse since then. Government funds and benefits have made a man in the household unnecessary. And, of course, those most affected are our most vulnerable: the children. The Annie E. Casey Foundation's "Kids Count" reports that in 2019, our home state of Louisiana ranked 50th in Economic Well-Being (with 28% of children in poverty), 48th in Education (with 74% of fourth graders not proficient in reading), 42nd in Health, and 48th in Family & Community (with 45% of children in single-parent homes and 20% of children living in high poverty neighborhoods).[7] For these statistics it is important to note that Louisiana has a high concentration of black communities (as do many southern states).

Many children in a generationally under-resourced neighborhood suffer to some degree from Adverse Childhood Experiences (A.C.E.) and resulting chronic stress. A.C.E.s in the home and neighborhood include verbal, physical, sexual, emotional abuse and neglect; mental illness, alcoholism, drug addiction in homes, divorced parents; and incarcerated family

---

[6] Census Bureau data, cited in Walter Williams' op-ed in the *Baton Rouge Advocate,* July 18, 2019.

[7] The Annie E. Casey Foundation, *2019 Kids Count Data Book: State Trends in Child Well-Being,*
https://www.aecf.org/m/resourcedoc/aecf-2019kidscountdatabook-2019.pdf, 53–55, 57.

members. A.C.E.'s reflects social, economic, mental, emotional, physical and spiritual poverty. Under the chronic stress of A.C.E.s, children's little bodies are flooded with adrenaline and cortisol. Blood flows to their brains are reduced and diverted to their big muscles to aid "fight or flight." The stress is constant and seems like it will never relent. It is as if a car engine has been placed in neutral and revved up at high RPM forever. Not only is the health of these children affected, but all attempts at right thinking, caring, and doing are hampered too. Their brains are in a fog and survival is their highest value. One result of this is an "achievement gap" in education, where children experiencing chronic stress start school behind and fall further and further behind. The fight or flight response to everything in their lives and at school becomes a habit that ultimately shapes their character. Tragically, these A.C.E. strongholds are being generationally passed down in homes and neighborhoods. If a child is afflicted with more than one A.C.E., they are disadvantaged; if they are afflicted with four or more, their life expectancy is radically reduced. Blessed is the child whose development is not hindered by A.C.E.'s, or the child who comes from an active family of faith that are less affected by A.C.E.'s.

For many people, a continual degradation of their dignity results in an identity crisis. This reality is especially prevalent in our generationally under-resourced families and neighborhoods. Too often, afflicted children normalize this loss of dignity and identity at the very youngest of ages. Of all the areas where a person might be poor, this loss of dignity for generations is our deepest poverty.

CHAPTER 2

POVERTY

Then God said, "Let us make mankind in our image, in our likeness..." So God created mankind in His own image, in the image of God He created them; male and female He created them. (Genesis 1:26a, 27, NIV)

Introduction: Poverty and the Dignity of Man

Every human being, as created, is a reflection of God's glory and is worthy of respect and love. The imago Dei forms a solid foundation and understanding for mankind's worth. Our worth is not established on our being rich or poor, but on our being created in the image and likeness of God. For Jews and Christians this identity should be foundational in all our relationships. After the Fall, however, the image of God became difficult to discern in the world and now must be seen and experienced by faith in the Word and Spirit of God. It is our true image and likeness that Christ came to reveal to us by becoming like us and making it possible for us to become like Him again. Thus, He loves, frees, and empowers believers to be the humble light in a dark and broken world—the same world that produces poverty at all levels, crushes human dignity, and blinds us to our true identity in Him. So, in order to understand how our God-given dignity and identity is diminished, it is important to understand poverty—not only what it is, but its cause as well.

What is Poverty?

Poverty is a lack of resources, and generational poverty is a lack of edifying resources for generations. There are 6 Key Resources required for human development: 1) Social Resources, 2) Economic Resources, 3) Mental Resources, 4) Emotional Resources, 5) Physical Resources, and interwoven throughout these edifying resources are 6) Spiritual Resources.

And, for a person to become whole, they must be both 'Capable' and 'Caring' in these 6 Key Resource Categories.

The Poor in Scripture

The Bible speaks about widows, the fatherless ("orphans" in the New Testament), aliens, and the lazy as being poor. Today, "widows" could also represent our single mothers. We still have the fatherless in our midst, as well as aliens who are marginalized because they are seen as outsiders. And, of course, we still have lazy people.

So what are we to do? Jesus famously said, "You will always have the poor among you" (John 12:8, NIV; also in Mark 14:7). Jesus was drawing from Deuteronomy 15:11 (NIV), where God says, "There will always be poor people." Yet in Deuteronomy 15:4 (NIV), God says, "There need be no poor people among you." Verse 11 seems to contradict verse 4—until we look a little closer. Deuteronomy 15:4 is stating that there should be no poor among His chosen people whom He has richly blessed and follow His commands. But outside God's family and reign, out in the land, there will always be poor people to whom we ought to be open-handed.

According to Deuteronomy 15:4, "There need be no poor people among you." That is, there should be no marginalized, needy widows, single moms, fatherless, orphans, aliens, or lazy in our churches today. There should be no needy persons among the church members who are richly blessed with "every spiritual blessing in Christ" (Ephesians 1:3, NIV). This ideal was modeled to us in the early church: "There were no needy persons among them" (Acts 4:34a, NIV).

Jesus reinforces the foundational principle of human dignity when He says, "Truly I tell you, whatever you did for one of the least of these brothers and sisters of mine, you did for me" (Matthew 25:40, NIV). Jesus is not only talking about the judgment of the nations on the basis of how they treat "these brothers of mine" (the Jews); he is also reinforcing the inherent dignity of mankind and saying that the physical and spiritual are inseparable. Like Jesus, we should have concern for the poor; and we should especially intervene with all our resources when poverty becomes generational. Without such intervention, those families who have known only poverty for decades have almost no hope for the recognition of their dignity or for the kind of life this country offers the resourced. It is simply not right or just to allow poverty to exist generation after generation.

Features of Poverty

How we view poverty dictates how we have historically attempted to alleviate poverty. If we see poverty as a lack of money, then our solutions will be financial in nature. If we see poverty as poor health, then our solution will be better health care. If we see poverty as a lack of education, then our solution will be educational reform. If we see poverty as a lack of housing, then we will build houses. Many times, we see poverty through the lens of the gifts *we* possess, rather than seeing poverty holistically. Thus, the saying, "If the only tool you hold in your hand is a hammer, you tend to see every problem as a nail" (Abraham Maslow).

In order to arrive at a fuller understanding of poverty, there are several characteristics that we ought to take into account:

Poverty is relative. A rich man who lives in a rich neighborhood with financially (economically) richer neighbors may not consider himself rich. An unhealthy man may not fully see his physical poverty if surrounded by sicker people. A financially poor man who lives alongside his poorer neighbors may not see himself as poor. But a physically or financially or spiritually poor man knows he is poor when he stands next to one who is rich in these things.

Poverty can be situational or generational in nature. A person in situational poverty may have temporarily lost his job, but have the resources to gain additional training or another job. A person in generational poverty does not possess or have access to the resources necessary to escape poverty. People who have been in poverty for more than one generation typically lack resources due to broken relationships with the resourced. There are no people in their lives capable of helping—no mentors, no role models, no one to point them to where or how the necessary resources can be accessed. Thus, generational poverty is self-perpetuating.

Poverty is a lack of edifying resources and is multifaceted. The symptoms of poverty point to a root lack of various resources, a lack which holds a person back from developing fully and achieving meaning and purpose in life. The 6 specific resources that are missing in generational poverty can be a mix of social, economic, mental, emotional, physical, and throughout all, spiritual resources. Besides the obvious, they include role models, wise mentors, social and workplace etiquette, work ethic, good character, food, safety and security, sense of belonging, self-esteem, whole families, wise and healthy life choices, God's grace, faith, truth, love, righteousness, justice, peace, etc. A generational poverty of resources ultimately depletes human dignity, a situation which is not right or just in light of man's inherent dignity.

Because poverty is multifaceted, it is not always easy to say who is rich and who is poor. For example, a financially rich man can be poor physically, socially, spiritually, or educationally. A spiritually rich man can be poor educationally, financially, socially, or physically—and so on. A multifaceted approach is required not only to understand but also to alleviate poverty and close the achievement gap.

Finding the Causes of Poverty

Some say a lack of education (mental development) leads to poverty. But education is not sufficient by itself to make a person whole. What happens if a trained and educated person is physically impoverished and cannot get to work? What about the educated man in your office who has a hard, cold heart? The heartless man may be hired for what he knows, but ultimately fired for who he is. As Wall Street has illustrated on occasion, highly educated people with hard hearts can cause much harm because they are spiritually, emotionally, or relationally (social resources) poor. The theory that a lack of education (mental resources) causes poverty is partially true, but it is not the silver bullet our culture currently touts. A lack of heart is a depleted resource just as much as a lack of education.

Some say a lack of healthcare or housing leads to poverty. But the same holds true here. Developing one or the other resource without "heart" development is not sufficient to solve the problem of poverty. On the other hand, what happens when someone has a huge heart, but lacks the mental and/or physical development to attain and keep a job? The spiritual development of the heart is important indeed, but it is not the silver bullet either.

The point is this: The solution for poverty is not found in any one part of human life, but in the whole of all the parts.

We tend to look only at the physical when we attempt to understand poverty. But the outcomes we can physically measure are, in reality, merely symptoms of poverty. Symptoms are great indicators and will point us to the root issues of poverty only if we, as a culture, care enough to swim upstream to truly understand and address the core issues. But if we come to poverty thinking we know it all, then our minds will be closed to learning the realities of poverty —and especially to understanding our *own* poverty. We may look rich on the outside, but the Lord sees when we are poor on the inside. ("You say, 'I am rich ... I need nothing', not realizing that you are wretched, pitiful, poor, blind, and naked." (Rev. 3:17)

Poverty of the Mind, Heart, and Body

Poverty can also be broken down in terms of the mind, heart, and body. Poverty of the mind leads to a lack of mental ability, self-control, education, knowledge, and training. Poverty of the body inhibits a person from going to work or staying at work. Mother Teresa once described the poverty of the heart as the "homelessness of the heart," which is "America's deepest poverty of all."[8] Poverty of the heart is a spiritual poverty that manifests itself in all of the key resources. . There is a poverty of the heart when a person feels alone and unknown in the world. If someone simply does not care about or respect the dignity of his fellow man, he has a poverty of the heart too.

Poverty of the mind and heart is harder to see than physical poverty, but it is just as real. If there is someone in your church who feels alone, your church is impoverished. If the church does not actively care about lifting the burdens and closing the gaps of the poor in their own community, the church is impoverished. If someone who lives in your home feels unknown and unloved, you

---

[8] Mother Teresa, *Loving Jesus* (Servant Publications, 1991), 3.

have poverty under your own roof. For wholeness' sake, believers must humbly approach poverty with an open mind and heart. Allowing God to break the hard ground around our heart and touch its soft spot.

The Root Cause of Poverty

The root cause of poverty is not so much physical as it is metaphysical. At the deepest level, poverty (as a recovered alcoholic knows) is a symptom of a deeper spiritual problem. The problem with concerning oneself only with the symptoms of poverty is that the issue itself is not visible. So many people, because they are not properly trained, cannot discern the true cause of poverty. Understanding the root cause is crucial because it allows us to more effectively discover solutions to poverty.

Steve Corbett and Brian Fikkert, in their book *When Helping Hurts*, summarize Bryant Myers' analysis of the root cause of poverty:

"Bryant Myers, a leading Christian development thinker, argues that in order to diagnose the disease of poverty correctly, we must consider the fundamental nature of reality, starting with the Creator of that reality. Myers notes that the Triune God is inherently a relational being, existing as three-in-one from all eternity. Being made in God's image, humans are inherently relational as well. Myers explains that before the fall, God established four foundational relationships for each person: a personal relationship with God, with self, with others, and with the rest of creation…These relationships are the building blocks for all of life. When they are functioning properly, humans experience the fullness of life that God intended, because we are being what God intended us to be."[9]

Consequently, Myers concludes that when any or all of these foundational relationships are not functioning individually and in unison with the others, poverty will exist. Thus we learn that ***poverty is caused by our broken relationships with God, self, neighbors, and creation. In our broken relationships, God's edifying resources do not flow vertically from Him to us or horizontally from us to our neighbor.***

Let's flesh out these concepts using a metaphor. In football there is a head coach and team. The team is a diverse group that have freely come together to play the game of football. In spending time with each other, they develop respectful relationships with one another. In these relationships, edifying and empowering resources begin to flow. To further mobilize the individuals into a true team, the coach casts a Super Bowl vision and a pathway (mission) to achieve this vision that the team can excitedly embrace and mobilize around. The coach begins constantly assessing the team's skills and fills the gaps by whatever means he has. He begins inspiring teamwork to motivate his team to achieve their Super Bowl goal. He must be able to provide all edifying resources they may need to become all they can be as a powerful Super Bowl team. Because of their respect for and belief in their Coach, the team rallies around his every word. They obediently do what he says for their team's benefits and rewards. They know they need their Coach to achieve their

---

[9] Steve Corbett and Brian Fikkert, When Helping Hurts: How to Alleviate Poverty Without Hurting the Poor…and Yourself (Chicago: Moody Publishers, 2012), 54.

goal. The Coach, in turn, respectfully shows tough-love to his team by teaching, rebuking, correcting, and training them in harmony towards their common goal. He raises the bar by telling them that without pain, there is no gain. He is not so much teaching as he is training and building their character, for he knows the going will be tough. In the mobilizing of the Super Bowl team, they must also highly respect each other and respect what each player uniquely adds to the team. The team may have initially assembled as a bunch of individuals with individual agendas, but under the Coach's rule, the team grants the Coach place over themselves and respectfully places their teammates over themselves too. They are not only in right and respectful relationships with the Coach (vertical relationships), but also with each other (horizontal relationships). As time goes on, the team acts more and more as one. They develop unity in their diversity. In this, they find a power that none could ever individually possess. As they see their team's work ethic produce fruit, their faith builds in their Coach, his tough-love system, and themselves, and this faith empowers the team to produce a Super Bowl win. They know they may not succeed, but they are giving their Super Bowl vision their best shot for the team's glory. But what happens when a team has broken relationships with their Coach? What happens when a team has broken relationships with each other? In reality, a broken relationship affects the whole team. When relationships are broken either with the Coach or within the team, there will exist a brokenness in both unless all relationships are quickly reconciled. The result of a team's broken relationships is a POOR team with no chance of success. The same holds true of our relationships with God and each other. Our broken relationships lead to poverty in our lives and commUNITY.

To summarize, the root cause of poverty is our four broken relationships with God, self, neighbor, and creation. To go even deeper, our broken relationships are the result of idolatry.

Idolatry

If one loves and values anything over God, then his heart will become impoverished. Anything that competes with God for our first love is an idol. This includes love of money, self, one's group, church, and even family. Man will do anything over and against God and neighbor to embrace his idol. Idols reflect man's misplaced loves of the heart.

Unfortunately, too few people today believe they have idols. Their picture of idolatry stems from the Old Testament—they imagine people worshipping foreign gods or carved images. But an idol is anything we place our trust in ahead of God. Do you put your trust in your finances? You have an idol! Do you put your trust in your spouse and kids? You have an idol! Sex, alcohol, drugs, your job, your power or position, your image? You have an idol! And, of course, the one idol we all share is what Oswald Chambers calls "my right to myself." God has a good plan for our lives and wants to be in control. But instead, we say "I want to be in control of my life." That is why Jesus said, "If you want to be my disciple, you must deny yourself."

The first two of the Ten Commandments state, "You shall have no other gods before Me" and "you shall not make idols" (Exodus 20; Deuteronomy 5). In other words, "Put God first."

If one values anything over God, he has become an idolater, and he is spiritually poor. He will break relationships with both

God and others to hang on to his idol. Furthermore, idolatry leads to oppression, which leads to injustice, which leads to poverty. Idolatry necessarily breaks relationships with God, self, and neighbor, and lead to oppressions, poverty, and a lack of resource flow. Idolatry, since it is a misplaced love, is a heart issue.

Poverty of the heart is America's deepest poverty and God's great concern. Simply stated, America is a culture of -holics who love almost everything more than God, self, and neighbors. We might say that America's "Holy Trinity" is Materialism, Ethnocentrism, and Individualism. Materialism is loving, trusting, and giving place to things, money, etc. more than God. In our Temple of Materialism and on its altar, we sacrifice God. Material things become our center. Ethnocentrism is loving, trusting, and giving place to our social, economic, political, or racial group over our neighbor (who is not like us). In our Temple of Ethnocentrism and on its altar, we sacrifice our neighbors. Our group becomes our center. Individualism is loving, trusting, and giving place to myself more than God. In our Temple of Individualism and on its altar, we sacrifice our true selves. We become self-centered and foolish.

Our cultural idols create systematic divisions, broken relationships, oppressions and injustices that create poverty socially, economically, mentally, emotionally, physically and in all spiritually. Our American Trinity culture unwittingly and innocently drive our social, economic, government, and religious systems. As prophets and addicts know, idolatry is a constant battle and our cultural idols are most hard to break.

The antidote to America's Holy Trinity requires a spiritual solution that is given to us in Jesus' Greatest Commandments to wholeheartedly love God, neighbor, and self (Matthew 22:37–40).

In other words, the antidote to America's Holy Trinity is Jesus' Way of love, which leads to the manifestation of the Kingdom of God on earth as it is in heaven.

On a practical level the best proven way to break the spiritual grip of any idol under these 3 big idol categories, is to follow and work the biblical principles offered in Celebrate Recovery's 12 Step Christ Centered Program.

In the first three steps of this proven 12 Step Program we are to: 1) Admit, 2) Submit and 3) Commit ... which begins our transformational journey towards wholeness... Resulting in the Revival of Christian life, individually and collectively. Let the work begin......

1. Admit that we are powerless over our idolatry—that our lives are out of our control because we have centered our lives around our misplaced loves (idols) that drive us.
2. Submit. Come to understand that our idols blind and deafen us to reality and believe that a Power greater than ourselves, who is Jesus Christ and His word in us, will restore the hope of wholeness.
3. Commit. Make a decision to turn our will and our lives over to the love, will and purpose of our Savior & Lord (choose to be Christ Centered in both word and Holy Spirit).

NOTE: Celebrate Recovery's 12 Step Program only works if you and your church work it. It is not for people who need or want it, but for those who will admit, submit and commit to working it. Making disciples of Christ entails teaching, rebuking, correcting and training a follower to do what they do not want to do, so they can become who they are meant to be.

Christians and Poverty Alleviation

The Biblical Solution to Poverty

In order to alleviate poverty without causing further harm, we must heed Jesus' commands. First and foremost, Jesus tells us to remove the log from our own eye so that we can see clearly (Luke 6:41–42). Let us see our idols clearly and not be blind to the fact of our own poverty in God's eyes. After all, the blind cannot lead the blind (Luke 6:39).

Instead of entering the poor man's life as a savior, we must clearly see our own poverty and humbly enter with the intentions of becoming friends. In friendship, the rich and the poor have much to offer each other. To illustrate this, Jesus tells the story of the rich man and Lazarus, who could not fathom what each could offer the other. Yet as the story reveals, the rich man and the poor man had everything to offer each other (Luke 16:19–31). In this world, the poor man, who was spiritually rich, was in a desperate temporal situation; and the rich man, who was spiritually poor, was in a most dangerous eternal situation. While they were on earth, neither could fathom what the poor man had to offer the rich man. Only after they both died did they realize that the poor man in heaven had everything to offer the rich man who now cried out from Hades. Only in building bridges of friendship in this world could they have lovingly exchanged their physical and spiritual gifts and become whole.

If we are to love those who are different than us in the way Jesus commands, we must learn to approach others humbly, even if we do not receive love and kindness in return. Jesus tells us that we will receive no benefit for loving those who already love us, because even sinners do that (Luke 6:32). On the other hand, by loving those who are unlike us, we work for the wholeness of both our neighbors and ourselves.

When believers love God with total obedience to His Word and Spirit in them (i.e., when we are centered in Christ), we stop relying on our material things and rely more and more on the love, freedom, and power of God in us. In reliance on God, our cultural idol of materialism begins to die. When we intentionally love our neighbor who is not like us, we begin to think about others and not place our group above other groups of people. As we love our neighbors, our cultural idol of ethnocentrism and racism dies away. Through loving God and others wholeheartedly, we begin to gain the character of Jesus and thus begin to truly love ourselves by acquiring His wisdom (Proverbs 19:8, NLT). In loving ourselves as God intends us to love ourselves, our hearts refocus on God and others; we begin dying to our false, fallen self and discovering who we truly are created to be in Christ. In rightly loving ourselves, our cultural idol of individualism begins to die. **In other words, our obedience to Jesus' Greatest Commandments demolishes our American Holy Trinity** (i.e., Individualism, Materialism, and Ethnocentrism) that breaks relationships, oppresses, and creates poverty.

After honestly looking in the mirror and understanding the blessings we receive by loving those not like ourselves (especially the poor), we must learn to discern and evaluate the situation of the poor. If we attempt to teach a man who is hungry to fish, he will become frustrated and mad. If we feed a man a fish (i.e., give him relief) when he really needs to be learning to fish (i.e., he needs development), then we may be guilty of creating dependency. What happens when a man learns how to fish, yet is told he cannot fish in the pond? It does not do him any good to know how to fish if he is not allowed to fish. Developing a person to become self-sufficient is the goal, and it may require him to learn not only how to fish and earn a piece of the pond, but even how to care for the pond and the community of fishermen (empowerment). Understanding these distinctions is necessary to understanding the two basic types of nonprofits: **Relief** and **Development** (or Empowerment). Most impoverished people today in America require long-term, relational Development, yet are receiving Relief from government, churches, and businesses that actually causes harm in the name of good. Except in the case of the physically and mentally incapable, **relief** must be short term, or dependent and entitled attitudes will quickly develop. **Development** should begin when relief ends and should be completed when a man is empowered to stand and walk on his own, possessing his rightful dignity.

How Do Christians Misunderstand Poverty?

Glen Kehrein spoke at the Annual Christian Community Development Association Conference held in New Orleans in 2004 about the fundamental differences between liberal and conservative white protestant theologies. This divide began right after the Civil War and involved a split in the mainline Protestant denominations over the issue of slavery along north/south lines. And this is his explanation of the differences.

The liberal church, due to the strong influence of the enlightenment philosophies of the day, experienced a paradigm shift. They began to believe the Bible to be a good book to follow and that Jesus was a good man to imitate. Thus, the liberal church began to see righteousness as "loving people" which is manifested through their social action. This became known as a Social Gospel. The liberal church saw the Kingdom of God as a just and present Kingdom here on earth and the purpose of this Social Gospel is to minister to "the least of these" who are poor. The liberal church's mission became one of social activism that leads them towards their overall vision of social redemption. So, WWJD if he was a white, liberal Protestant? Jesus would, in love, intervene socially and bring justice to the poor and feed the hungry.

The conservative church stayed true to their original beliefs that the Bible is historically accurate and inspired by God, and it is only through Jesus that one is "saved." Thus, the conservative church saw righteousness as "loving God," which is seen as being spiritually devout, pious, and virtuous. The conservative church saw the Kingdom of God as righteous and future, and their Gospel purpose deals with an individual's spirituality. The conservative church's mission then is personal evangelism and that leads them towards their ultimate vision of personal salvation. This became known as the Personal Gospel. So WWJD if he was a white, conservative Protestant? Jesus would in truth intervene spiritually (evangelism) and save the lost.

After the 1930s, these two Protestant Christian camps became diametrically opposed to each other due to obtaining their truths from different sources [scientific truth versus biblical truth]. While each side calls themselves Christian, the Gospel of Jesus Christ was split into the Social Gospel and the Personal Gospel. Their debate stances are constant arguments about truth versus love.

Thus, the liberal side of the Protestant church envisions poverty as being caused by a broken Social Gospel (not loving thy neighbor). The conservative side of the Protestant church envisions poverty as being caused by a broken Personal Gospel (not loving God). One side sees poverty as being caused by social injustice, while the other points to personal irresponsibility. But according to a truly biblical perspective, poverty is caused by both social and personal gods. The American white church often misunderstands poverty because it has embraced one-sided theologies.

In the black Protestant churches a fuller gospel is usually preached.

So, Why Is Jesus So Concerned About Poverty?

Jesus is concerned about our hearts. He is concerned about our love of idols that causes broken relationships with God, self, and neighbors. Poverty's broken relationships, both individually and collectively, are rooted in our hearts. When idolatry causes broken relationships, God's blessings and resources cannot flow either vertically from God to us, or horizontally from us to others. A full understanding of idolatry follows broken relationships to the deeper issues of our hearts. This understanding comes from our struggle to faithfully love in harmony with God's will (agape-sacrificial love).

Thus poverty is actually caused by our deeper heart issue that leads us to break the Greatest Commandments, which were first given by God to Moses (in Deuteronomy 6:5 and Leviticus

19:18) and reiterated by Jesus in each gospel. After the Pharisee recited the Greatest Commandments in Mark 12:34 (NIV), Jesus said, "You are not far from the Kingdom of God."

In light of Jesus' Greatest Commandments, why do you think Jesus is so concerned for the poor among us? Jesus is particularly concerned about *why* the poor are poor. Jesus is concerned about the symptoms of poverty, but He is even more concerned with the sinful condition of our hearts that causes poverty. To be in the Kingdom of God where there is no poverty is to live under the Rule of God. Again, to fully under-stand, we must obediently stand-under the King's Rule of Love.

To conclude, why should Christians pay special attention to the poor? The poor are the visible manifestation of our broken spiritual relationships with God, self, and neighbors. Poverty is the visible sign that we are not living within God's revealed will for us (summed up in Jesus' Greatest Commandments). Poverty is the red flag, the visible signal that we in our community have misplaced loves (idols/gods) and are disobedient to Jesus' Greatest Commandments. Poverty's many facets point to man's lack of love. Thus, poverty anywhere in a community results in poverty *everywhere* in a community.

In God's revealed will for us, the Greatest Commandment, which is love, is essential in creating and maintaining right relationships that will alleviate poverty. Edifying resources rightly flow in God's loving relationships. It is true what John M. Perkins says: "love is our last battle". And love begins with the revelation that Christ first loves me! This revelation goes beyond our need to be loved by people to our deepest need to first know and be loved by our Savior and Lord.

The great antidote to poverty is to obediently choose to love

God, self, and neighbor with all our hearts, minds, bodies, and souls. Christ calls us to move intimately into the lives of the poor, just as He did, to lovingly reconcile people and redeem what has been lost or broken. The Word Himself became flesh and moved into our neighborhood to reconcile and redeem what is broken and lost of the Kingdom. The Family of God, as Ambassadors of Christ, are called to provide for, protect, teach, and love our economically and spiritually poor neighbors where we and they live. Consequently, we need to give serious thought about how to go about becoming such a neighbor. And as members of God's family, we look to the "firstborn," Jesus Christ, for guidance.

Jesus gives believers the directions for achieving greatness when He says, in effect, "The Way up is down" (see Mark 10:35–45). Jesus' bias is downward towards the poor and broken. But God's bridges are not built to the poor for one-way traffic, but two-way traffic—we benefit too! Humbly going down to, standing alongside, and loving the poor is the best way for Christ-centered Christians to both grow up into Christ-like character and alleviate poverty. Knowing this, Christ Jesus basically shouts to us, "Go down…the Way up is down!" He teaches us that whether we are rich or poor, we should all seek to achieve greatness by serving the lowly —not by aggrandizing ourselves. This can be done only when we rely on the leading and power of the Holy Spirit and place total trust in Him and His word.

Jesus called a little child to come to him. He stood the child in front of the followers. Then he said, "The truth is, you must change your thinking and become like little children. If you don't do this, you will never enter God's kingdom. The greatest person in God's kingdom is the one who makes himself humble like this child. Whoever accepts a little child like this in my name is accepting Me" (Matthew 18:2–5, ERV). Just as a child is dependent on his or her father, so too must we be. As we reach out to the generationally poor child, we recognize that we ourselves are children of God who must submit to and trust Him if we are to love as He loves.

The generationally poor child holds the golden key to our wholeness.

"Let the little children come to me .... for the Kingdom of God belongs to such as these." (Luke 18:16, Matthew 19:14, Mark 10:14)

CHAPTER 3

LOVE

Unlike "relief," a ministry grounded in "development" is difficult and time consuming. No one who spends any length of time in such work can do it in their own strength but must rely on God and His Church. This is especially true when it comes to working with those in generational poverty. Most often, it is so difficult to get off to a good start that frustration can set in. The only way to make headway is to commit to sacrificially loving the neighbors before us—to choose to put their needs and well-being ahead of ours.

Once believers are following the Agape Way of becoming like Christ, they come to understand that balance and wholeness are achieved by paying attention to God's "both-and" truths. Throughout the Bible, rather than "either/or" God's wisdom frequently leads us to view things from a "both-and" perspective. Job's friend summed up this truth when he said, "True wisdom has two sides" (Job 11:6, NIV).

Our sovereign Father is *both* our Savior *and* our Lord. God is *both* a God of "Release" *and* a God of "Development and Empowerment." When we consider the revealed Will of God, we see God's Greatest Commandments directing us to love *both* God *and* neighbor, to love *both* the King *and* His Kingdom *both* on earth *and* in heaven. When we look at man, we see his deep need for *both* freedom *and* power. We also see man's deeper need *both* to be loved *and* to love. God promises to *both* free *and* empower believers with *both* forgiveness from sin *and* the indwelling power of His Spirit and Word under the New Covenant. Faithful believers are *both* graciously released *and* empowered to be loved and to love.

Paul teaches theology (the way God thinks) in the first half of each of his New Testament letters. In the second half, he teaches us the practical application of God's thinking. In *both* Word *and* Spirit, we are to *both* prayerfully meditate on God's thoughts daily *and* actively live out God's Word in our lives. That is, we are to *both* pray *and* act. When we do this, our prayers will move us into right actions, our right actions will move us back to the feet of Christ in prayer, and prayer again moves us back into action. The "both-and" prayer-action cycle repeats itself in our lives as we conform to the image of Jesus.

Living up on the Sacred Pathway (the Narrow Gate—see Matthew 7:13–14) keeps man from falling into *either* the left ditch *or* the right ditch. When upon the Sacred Pathway, we find ourselves living between worlds with other peacemaking ambassadors of Christ. Staying on the pathway requires constant teaching, rebuking, correcting, and training in right thinking, right caring, and right doing (2 Timothy 3:16–17). In striving for the Kingdom of God and His character likeness (Matthew 6:33), we discover our wholeness, purpose, and true identity as creatures of God.

In Scripture, God teaches us that *both* the physical *and* spiritual are a unity in the human person. Secular man creates a dichotomy between the physical and the spiritual. As a result,

Sundays often do not carry over into Mondays and the work week. But the Ten Commandments deal with our relationships *both* with God *and* with man. The spiritual Word became physical flesh. In creating a dichotomy between the physical and spiritual, Christians become bad witnesses for Christ, for their faith is not lived out to the fullest extent and they are able to bear little to no fruit. Only when *both* the physical *and* the spiritual are embraced in a unity will our faith produce fruit that will last. In making the invisible visible, faithful Christians become the living proof of a loving God in a broken and hurting world.

A whole person can be described as being *both* capable *and* caring, *both* truthful *and* loving, *both* Word-centered *and* Spirit-centered. He knows how to *both* catch fish *and* care for the pond and other fishermen, he embraces *both* a personal gospel *and* a social gospel, and he loves *both* God *and* neighbor. A whole person simultaneously sees the world *both* as-it-truly-is *and* as-it-should-be. As a bird needs a right wing *and* a left wing to fly, a whole person requires both sides too. A whole person needs "both-and" and is incomplete, irrational, and frustrated if constantly fighting his or her own shadow in the "either-or." For example, people who stand on the side of the truth are constantly fighting the people who make a stand on the side of love, and vice versa. Both sides are incomplete in themselves, and they must acknowledge and let go of their shadows (i.e., idols) to become whole and balanced. Christian people need to be taught and trained in the "both-and," because our natural, foolish worldview is generally limited to the "either-or." Beyond the fork in the road, God's wisdom is found in the "both-and." After all, whole people who are both capable and caring make up whole families, who make up whole churches, whole neighborhoods, and whole communities. The Kingdom of God is made up of Kingdom people who reflect the whole identity of Christ.

Agape Love

"'You must love the Lord your God with all your heart, all your soul, and all your mind.' This is the first and greatest commandment. A second is equally important: 'Love your neighbor as yourself.' The entire law and all the demands of the prophets are based on these two commandments." (Matthew 22:37–40, NLT)

Mother Teresa often said that our deepest human need is to love and to be loved. Generally speaking, the depth of our understanding of love will determine the depth at which we live our lives. For example, if a person embraces an understanding of love determined by feeling, their lives will reflect a certain shallowness, self-focus, softness, and flakiness. On the other hand, if they see love as a choice that is divine and sacrificial, they will reflect this by giving themselves nobly to something larger than themselves. Why do some people choose to live at this deeper level? 1 John 4:19 answers this question: "We love because He first loved us" (NIV). It is when God reveals His unconditional love to us that we choose to obey Him by leading lives of sacrificial love for others.

In the Old Testament, the Hebrew word *hesed* is used to describe a love that places others above oneself. In the New Testament, the Greek word *agape* is used to convey the same idea of a sacrificial love. This special type of Judeo-Christian agape love, "whether exercised toward the brethren, or toward men generally, is not an impulse from the feelings, it does not alway run with the natural inclinations, nor does it spend itself only upon those for whom some affinity is discovered."[10] Agape love originates from God. According to His design, it is also the defining characteristic of born-again believers and the primary expression of their faith (Gal. 5:6).

Jesus specifically defines agape love as being sacrificial in John 15:13 (NIV): "Greater love has no one than this: to lay down one's life for one's friends." Holy Scripture describes God as being the true essence of agape love. As 1 John 4:7–8 says, "Dear friends, let us love (agape) one another, for love comes from God. Everyone who loves has been born of God and knows God. Whoever does not love does not know God, because God is love" (NIV; see also 1 John 4:16). God's demonstration of sacrificial agape love is that Christ Jesus willingly chose us over Himself and made an atoning sacrifice for our sins (Ro. 5:8, 1 John 4:10). The Bible also tells us that without agape love, we are but resounding gongs and clanging cymbals. Because agape love is so essential to who God is, if we do not have it, we are nothing (1 Cor. 13:1–3).

As Christians, agape love is our daily duty. It is our most heroic, most noble, and highest calling—a very tough-love indeed. Paul enlightens believers to the fact that to live a sacrificial life is our true and proper act of worship: "Therefore, I urge you, brothers and sisters, in view of God's mercy, to offer your bodies as a living sacrifice, holy and pleasing to God—this is your true and proper worship" (Rom. 12:1, NIV). But we must always place this difficult calling in the context of God's faithful love to us. We

---

[10] "Love," in Vine's Complete Expository Dictionary of Old and New Testament Words.

only love because He first loved us. Scripture reassures us that God loves *all* mankind at the agape level, with none excluded: "For God so loved the world that He gave His one and only Son" (John 3:16, NIV).

The cross shows us Christ's great love. God's desire for this agape love to reign in our lives cannot be accomplished in one's own strength. It will require believers in their prayerful weakness to rely on God, His Word, and His Spirit every minute of every day to transform them and love through them. Agape love requires disciples to deny our false selves, take up our crosses daily, and follow Jesus (Luke 9:23). God knows who we are and desires to reveal our true identity (i.e., the imago Dei) to His faithful followers through His agape process. To die to the false and fallen self is to live (Mark 8:34–35; Matthew 16:25).

While agape love is the type of love most often referred to in the New Testament, it is not the only one. Another Greek word for love in the New Testament is *phileo* (verb). *Phileo* means "to have ardent affection and feeling—a type of impulsive love."[11] This is the natural, human type of love, feeling, and affection that we have for a friend, and is often defined as "brotherly love." *Phileo* is a love that man can naturally demonstrate in his own power.

One of the best places in Scripture to see the difference between *agape* and *phileo* loves is in a certain dialogue between Jesus and Peter. In John 21:15–16, Jesus asks Peter if he loves Him (*agapao*), and Peter responds three different times that he indeed loves Him (*phileo*). Later, after receiving the transforming

---

[11] "Love," in *Nelson's New Illustrated Bible Dictionary* (Nashville, TN: Thomas Nelson, 1995).

power of the indwelling Holy Spirit, Peter is empowered to genuinely demonstrate agape love by serving others throughout his lifetime and making the ultimate sacrifice in martyrdom.

God's agape love is one of the scarlet threads in Scripture. As we better understand it, we better stand-under commands like "offer your bodies as living sacrifices" (Romans 12:1) and "carry your cross daily" (Luke 9:23); and, through love, we begin to see the Word of Christ through the eyes and Spirit of Christ. Agape helps us understand our need both for having our sins mercifully forgiven and for the intimate indwelling power of the Holy Spirit (New Covenant grace) to help us follow Jesus' way of love. As we follow the Agape Way, we begin to understand and personally identify in the life-death-resurrection pattern of Christ Jesus that we are to walk in daily. Agape allows followers to intimately experience God as we faithfully serve and obey Him daily. Agape love becomes our great Christian identifier and our great transformer.

True agape love, as explained in the Bible, is not focused on oneself and one's feelings or emotions (*philia*), but chooses to be outwardly and intentionally focused on others, driven by the desire to rightly serve God by serving others. True agape love is beautifully described in 1 Corinthians 13:4–8 (NIV):

Love is patient, love is kind. It does not envy, it does not boast, it is not proud. It is not rude, it is not self-seeking, it is not easily angered, it keeps no record of wrongs. Love does not delight in evil but rejoices with the truth. It always protects, always trusts, always hopes, always perseveres. Love never fails.[12]

Agape love is to be our defining Christian characteristic, the expression of our faith in Christ (Galatians 5:6). As John 13:35 says, "Your [agape] love for one another will prove to the world that you are my disciples" (NLT). As disciples, agape love is not only our Great Transformer, but also our "Great and Noble Identifier." It is through our Savior and Lord's grace-faith-love character-building process that we begin to see in Whose image we were originally created before the Fall. The Agape Way means dying to our false self while being transformed into our true self as originally created in the image of God.

Below is a table summarizing the contrast between agape and secular love (adapted from *Robertson's Word Pictures of the New Testament)*:

Secular Love	Agape Love
Comes from the power of man	Comes from the power of the Spirit
Ultimately focused on the self	Focused on God and neighbor
Based on emotions	Based on a choice to obey God
Discriminatory and conditional	Non-discriminatory and unconditional
Often fails	Never fails

---

[12] As an exercise, replace "love" and "it" with your name in these verses above. Read these verses again with your name added. Can you see where God has some developing and empowering work to do in you and us?

To summarize, philia love is present even in secular man, who does not rely on God's indwelling power. Agape love is divine and requires that we die to ourselves. It can only be accomplished by relying on the power of Christ's indwelling Spirit and the guidance of God's Word. In Scripture, we are promised that even through our suffering God is developing a Christ-like character in us. This path to character development is the tough path of agape love.

"Therefore, since we have been justified by faith, we have peace with God through our Lord Jesus Christ. Through him we have also obtained access by faith into this grace in which we stand, and we rejoice in hope of the glory of God. More than that, we rejoice in our sufferings, knowing that suffering produces endurance, and endurance produces character, and character produces hope, and hope does not put us to shame, because God's love has been poured into our hearts through the Holy Spirit who has been given to us" (Romans 5:1–5, ESV).

"It helps to keep in mind the two-sided reality of the Christian life. On the one hand, we are complete in Christ (our acceptance with Him is secure). On the other hand, we are growing in Christ (we are becoming more and more like Him). At one and the same time we have both the status of kings and the duties of slaves. We feel both the presence of Christ and the pressure of sin. We enjoy the peace that comes from being made right with God, but we still face daily problems that often help us grow. If we remember these two sides of the Christian life, we will not grow discouraged as we face temptations and problems. Instead, we will learn to depend on the power available to us from Christ, who lives in us by the Holy Spirit."[13]

Once being justified by grace through faith, believers stand and rejoice in the hope of God's glory. In Romans 5:1–5, we are told that we should even rejoice in our suffering and struggles! Believers are promised that our struggles (like the football coach's "tough-love training") will produce endurance, and our endurance will produce Christ character, which will produce hope on the other side of our sufferings and struggles. This is all possible because God's agape love has been poured into our hearts by the Holy Spirit.

The Two Sides of the Love Coin

Note: Going forward, phileo will be spoken of as "mercy" (as demonstrated in our mercy relief ministries and charities) and agape will be spoken of as "tough-love" (as demonstrated in development ministries). One side of the love coin "releases," while the back side of the love coin "develops" and "empowers."

Conventionally, most people see only one side of love—mercy. As a result, mercy ministries offering relief proliferate in our society today. It seems that only a few people rightly see the other side of the love coin as being development and empowerment. Development ministries require "tough-love" and will not "do" for those who can do for themselves. "Tough-love" does not appear loving to many mercy folk, because it requires those who are loved to grow up into maturity, a process that

---

[13] Note on Rom. 5:1–5, *Tyndale's Life Application Study Bible* (Grand Rapids, MI: Zondervan, 2011), 1884.

involves much learning, struggle, and even suffering. As the result of our one-sided understanding of the love coin, there are few "tough-love" ministries devoted to speaking the truth in love. Most of our work, whether accomplished by religious organizations or secular organizations, is mercy work that does not go beyond "feeding fish."

Many of us have seen TV reality shows that deal with drug interventions. The loving family members confront their addict family member with the hard truth that they are withdrawing their mercy. They have come to the knowledge that their resources, although they are given out of mercy, have been enabling their loved one to continue down a self-destructive path. This tough-love rebuking and correcting does not feel loving to the addict and usually angers him or her. The tough-loving family is taking the big risk of losing their loved one by their decision to draw the line in the sand at his or her feet. Tough-lovers obviously love very much, but their love is not risk-free, comfortable, convenient, or feel-good. "Speaking the truth in love" is tough and difficult for many soft-hearted people to stomach.

The Catholic Traditions identify seven physical works of mercy: to feed the hungry, give drink to the thirsty, clothe the naked, shelter the homeless, visit the sick, visit the imprisoned, and (in the Book of Tobit) to bury the dead. These works, as their name implies, are mercy ministries that deal only with relief or release. Yet this is not to diminish their value. In the New Covenant, Christ's mercy is shown to us in His forgiveness of our sins (see Heb. 8:12, NIV: "For I will forgive their wickedness and will remember their sins no more"). Under His New Covenant mercy, God "releases" believers from their sin, lifting our burdens that we are incapable of lifting. In response, God calls us to show mercy to others. Mercy ministries and non-profits feed, give drink, clothe, shelter, visit the sick and imprisoned, and bury the dead. Mercy does for those who are incapable of doing for themselves.

Imagine that a man, bleeding to death, lies before us. Mercy steps up and says, "Yes, I will stop your bleeding." But when the bleeding stops, so should the mercy. Mercy is a short-term endeavor. When we habitually "feed fish" to the needy without a view to their long-term betterment, we often create dependency and even a strong sense of entitlement. This dependency and entitlement produce resentment in both the giver and the receiver poisoning the hearts of both and further dividing community. We thus cause harm to that individual, ourselves and the society in which we reside, in the name of doing good. Doing mercy without a mission and vision to quickly move towards developing and empowering the human being into self-sufficiency and wholeness causes harm. It expends resources unwisely and **distorts human dignity**. Mercy without tough-love expectations also inflates our mercy ministry businesses and, in the name of good, causes the poverty needle to move in the wrong direction. Thus, the saying, "The road to hell is paved with good intentions."

Most often the recipient of our mercy ministries is not bleeding to death. With no vision beyond mercy, our mercy ministries continue attending downstream to the symptoms of poverty rather than focusing resources on the root causes of the recipient's poverty upstream.

God's well-fare system is much different than our religious and government welfare systems that are focused almost exclusively on mercy. A two-sided system based on agape love quickly moves from relief to development. It maintains recognition of the dignity of man by also demanding of him and for him long-term, relational human development and empowerment. We must go beyond our current mercy-models of charity by also embracing the tough-love side of agape that develops and empowers people to ultimately take responsibility for their own lives, instead of enabling and harming them further. Tough-lovers are not there to "fix" the problem, but to embrace the problem as their own, knowing that when we faithfully embrace our neighbor's struggle, Christ's character is built in both us and our neighbor.

From Scripture, believers know that God is love (1 John 4:8, 16). We know that love is the essence of God. We know that God loves us. Then how do we understand God's love when He expelled Adam and Eve from the Garden? Or when God's Chosen People were enslaved in Egypt for 430 years and went on a forty-year wandering death march in the desert? Or when Moses was not allowed into the Promised Land? Or when the Kingdom of Israel was divided, prophets were killed, and God's people were carried into captivity? Or when God allowed His own Son to die? Is God mean and vengeful, or do we not understand the agape love of God correctly? Believers generally "get" the mercy side of God's love, but we often miss the tough-love side. Maybe we miss the tough-love message of our Lord because mercy "feels" good, but tough-love often doesn't. Under God's tough-love, His Spirit and Word are continuously teaching, rebuking, correcting, training, and disciplining His children to think rightly, care rightly, and do rightly in Christ. As a parent trains and develops his child through discipline, so also God trains and develops followers of Christ. As Proverbs 13:24 says, "He who withholds the rod of discipline hates his son, but he who loves him disciplines and trains him diligently and appropriately with wisdom and love" (AMP).

Against conventional wisdom, tough-love does not always feel good. It takes that kind love to allow a loved one to run out of rope in his life before coming to his senses. Remember that Jesus Christ and His Holy Spirit intervened in our lives to tell us the truth of who we truly are and bring us into a life of sanity.

Tough-love calls us to move beyond our feelings and then choose to die to ourselves by daily relying on God's truth, guidance, and power in us. Both mercy and tough-love are aimed at the reconciliation and redemption of our right and loving relationships with God, self, and neighbors. Yes, there will be suffering and death to our false self, but this should not cause us to lose hope. In our faithful Christian walk towards maturing in Christ, suffering is to be expected, and there is no place for the victim narrative of bondage and powerlessness. Suffering and struggles simply come with life—especially the Christian life. Yet followers of Christ are released and empowered to rejoice in our suffering, not because we enjoy it or deny its extent, but because we know that God is training us through it to become more like His Son. Christians also know by faith that neither suffering nor even death has the last word. By the great power of God, Christ was resurrected. For those who love Jesus Christ, there is always hope on the other side. 1 Peter 5:10 describes what we have to look forward to: "After you have suffered for a while, God Himself will make you perfect. He will keep you in the right way. He will give you strength. He is the God of all loving-favor and has called you through Christ Jesus to share His shining-greatness forever" (NLV).

Work and Love

Work is a sacred gift from God that was given to man l the Fall. According to God's design, work is a source of meaning and the recognition of dignity for human beings. He demonstrated this truth when He gave the Israelites His law of gleaning in Leviticus 19:9–10: "When you reap the harvest of your land, do not reap to the very edges of your field or gather the gleanings of your harvest. Do not go over your vineyard a second time or pick up the grapes that have fallen. Leave them for the poor and the foreigner" (NIV; see also Lev. 23:22). We see this practice played out in the book of Ruth (Ruth 2:3, NIV: "So she went out, entered a field and began to glean behind the harvesters").

The law of gleaning meant that landowners and harvesters were not to squeeze total production from their fields, but for love and dignity's sake to leave a portion for the poor. The poor in Old Testament times were to make their meager living by working to glean this portion. The person's dignity was recognized since he was able to take responsibility for his own life by work. Our question is this: how can we develop a vision to allow the poor and rich today to embrace their dignity, by some twenty-first-century equivalent to "gleaning," and to ultimately become self-sufficient through their work? "Where there is no vision [no redemptive revelation of God], the people perish," says Proverbs 29:18 (AMP). Today people are dying because of a lack of a redemptive vision. Mercy ministries need to remember the redemptive revelation from God that goes beyond conventional charity. Mercy ministries need God's bigger and deeper vision for tough-love development, and for this, they need a more comprehensive understanding of agape love.

Historically, mercy ministries often have a good beginning, but they are not deep and relational enough in their work and thus do not develop people to become whole. Instead of fostering loving relationships, they create dependent, entitled and resentful givers and recipients of charity. That is, mercy alone often undermines the true work of love. And as Reverend Charles Hill of Abbeville, Louisiana once wisely said to us, "If whatever we are doing does not end in love, we are simply wasting our time."

In the ministry world, instead of an integration of mercy and development, we often see tension build between people who value mercy and people who value tough-love. Each group of people has an incomplete, one-sided idea of biblical love. Thus, both the mercy folk and the tough-love folk move away from agape love that is the will of God toward what they personally feel is best. And all the while, people are perishing.

Dr. John M. Perkins, founder of Christian Community Development Association, once asked a group of us the big question, "How do we affirm the dignity of people, motivate them, while helping them to take responsibility for their lives?" Not many people have taken up the challenge. There are very few development and empowerment-based nonprofits that are working today to empower the poor. This is partially because lovingly developing and empowering people by building them up spiritually and economically is highly relational and requires commitment and energy. Like those raising up a child, development ministries must be in it for the long haul, slowly building up individuals into whole, capable, and caring people who will form healthy families, neighborhoods, and communities. This development-empowerment work that flows from agape love requires much more time, money, and prayer than short-term mercy relief. It takes us beyond "feeding fish" and requires us to carry our crosses daily, to die to our false self, and to come to the feet of Jesus before every action.

As we saw before, mercy ministries say, "Yes, I will help you stop the bleeding." Once the bleeding stops, tough-love ministries say, "No, I will not do for you what you can and should do for yourself—but I will be here with you always." This "no" response of tough-love is the "Iron Rule of Development." Only a small fraction of people in America are "bleeding to death," contrary to the messages of our media and "relief" businesses. The greatest need in America is not for more mercy ministries but for long-term, tough-love, development-empowerment ministries that are highly relational.

In summary, there is a two-sided reality of the Christian life. In Christ's mercy, He saved us when we were helpless to save ourselves. But God is not just a God of mercy, but also a God of development and empowerment who builds up His followers into His character likeness. Christ's Spirit is not simply doing "for" us so much as He is doing "with" and "in" us who faithfully follow Him. As a reflection of His character in our own works of love, we are not to do "for" those who can and should do for themselves, but "with" and "alongside" them.

Release and empowerment are two sides of the same coin. Both are required for a full expression of agape love. Love is the toughest stuff on earth. It requires that we faithfully obey God instead of depending on our feelings. But we can be assured that as we seek the wholeness of our neighbors, we discover our own wholeness in Christ Jesus.

CHAPTER 4

WHOLE PEOPLE, WHOLE COMMUNITY

The Beloved Whole Community

All people are born with the deep desire to live in what we call a "Beloved Whole CommUnity": a community that fulfills man's deepest needs to be loved and to love; a community of grace that is both freeing and empowering; a community that is faithfully anchored in the everlasting truth of Jesus' life, death, and resurrection and in the virtues of faith, hope, and love. In a Kingdom community, trusting and trustworthy people firmly stand together in the grace and truth of Christ and express their obedient faithfulness in agape love for God, self, and neighbor. Righteous character structures of right thinking, right caring, and right doing are built on the strong foundation of faithful love. The result is a just community characterized by peace, joy, and a *shalom* (wholeness) where nothing is lost or broken and there are no burdens and no gaps. This wholeness results in peace and joy in the power of the Spirit of Christ who is in and with us always. The character of the King and His Kingdom is embraced and emulated by all, and wisdom reigns. This Shalom Kingdom of God is our desired Beloved Whole CommUnity where we are all one in Christ our King.

How is this to be? Jesus Christ revealed the pathway to this Kingdom in His Greatest Commandments (Matthew 22:37–40). When we follow these commandments, God's freeing and empowering resources readily flow both vertically and horizontally in right and caring relationships between God, self, and neighbors. These divine resources reflect the character of our King and include grace, faithfulness and truth, love, righteousness, justice, and shalom (peace, wholeness, joy). These holistic resources flow down from the Trinity into our lives and the life of the community and conform us, His Body, to His image. As we acquire the wisdom and character of Jesus, we begin to love rightly and to discover our true identity. The tarnish on our souls resulting from the Fall is polished away, and God's love, peace, and joy begin to shine through. This relational vertical and horizontal flow within the Beloved Community is summed up in Scripture by the "fruit of the Spirit." Galatians 5:22–23 says, "But the fruit of the Spirit is love, joy, peace, patience, kindness, goodness, faithfulness, gentleness and self-control." Think about a community that is defined by these fruits. It would become quickly renowned; people inside and outside this community would call it blessed. Some would call it heaven on earth, a "Beloved Whole Community" where nothing is broken or lost.

When the fruits of the Spirit abound, resources begin to flow down from the Beloved Whole Community and out into its systems and families. These resources free people and develop and empower them to become righteous and loving role models, members of whole families, and respectful members of the community who exhibit social and workplace skills. The community experiences safety and security as well as healthcare, financial and mental resources, adequate shelter, life sustaining work, etc. Members of the Beloved Whole Community are safe, secure, capable, and caring, and they lead lives of meaning and purpose. They are whole people who in turn raise whole children.

How do we build such a community? We must follow Jesus' Agape Way, revealed to us in His Greatest Commandments. **We must love both the King and Kingdom**: that is, we must choose to love God, self, and neighbors with all our minds, hearts, and actions. When we do this, we will become whole people who make up whole communities. Furthermore, in whole communities, where resources and blessings flow with righteousness and justice, there will be no poor. In Deuteronomy 15:4–5, God instructs the Beloved Whole Community: "There should be no poor among you, for the Lord your God will greatly bless you in the land he is giving you as a special possession. You will receive this blessing if you are careful to obey all the commands of the Lord your God that I am giving you today" (NLT).

"BELOVED COMMUNITY"
"THY WILL BE DONE"

God's Empowering Resources Flow in Right and Caring Relationships

TRINITY
Faith — Love — Justice
Grace — Righteousness
Truth — Shalom
Holy Spirit & Word

BELOVED COMMUNITY
Faithfulnes — Love
Generosity — Kindness
Patience — Goodness
Peace — Gentleness
Joy — Self-Control

FAMILY
Emotional — Spiritual
Safety Net — Health
Etiquette — Financial
Role-Model — Mental

CHILD
Wholeness = Capable and Caring

Being Conformed to the Character Image of Jesus Christ

The Broken Community

With broken relationships, there can be no flow of spiritual resources from God. There is no grace, no faith in truth, no love, righteousness, or justice, and ultimately there can be no shalom. Instead of abundant life, there is poverty.

In a Broken Community, the idols of individualism, materialism, and ethnocentrism take precedence over God and neighbors. Individual relationships are broken. Man is now led by the flesh, the world's demands, and Satan himself, not by the Spirit and Word of God. He is far from the Kingdom of God. The dysfunctional behavior that results is described in Galatians: "The acts of the flesh are obvious: sexual immorality, impurity and debauchery; idolatry and witchcraft; hatred, discord, jealousy, fits of rage, selfish ambition, dissensions, factions and envy; drunkenness, orgies, and the like. I warn you, as I did before, that those who live like this will not inherit the kingdom of God" (Galatians 5:19–21, NIV).

These acts of the flesh are placed in direct contrast to the fruits of the Spirit (verses 22, 23) and reflect a Broken Community where there is no flow of spiritual, relational, and economic resources. Many families in a Broken Community are impoverished and broken. There is no safety or security, no righteous role models, no knowledge of social and workplace etiquette, no mental resources, no spiritual resources, no health resources, no self-sustaining work or work ethic, no adequate housing, no truth, no trust, no love, no respect for human dignity, no righteousness or justice, no shalom, no Christ-likeness, no wisdom. Raised in broken families, many children grow up bent, wounded, and stunted, with few resources to develop their minds and hearts. They often become incapable and uncaring adults with little to no truth or love to pass down to the next generation. As money makes money, poverty makes poverty. Broken relationships result in broken people, broken families, broken neighborhoods, broken communities, and broken nations. Across society, trust goes down while crime goes up. Under the chronic stress of living in such a community, God is often forgotten and His image is tarnished, resulting in feelings of worthlessness and shame. There is no hope of resurrection on either the rich or the poor side of town.

In a Broken Community, we are confused and easily misled by lies. No one takes responsibility, and blame abounds. People become passive, constantly fighting and arguing instead of leading courageously. Meanwhile, economic and spiritual poverty increases. The children suffer from a lack of divine resources; they develop emotional issues and become angry. As time goes on, this fallen state of affairs becomes normalized in the lives of the members of the community. The foundations of common-unity seem impossible to recover from.

"BROKEN COMMUNITY"
Poverty is Caused by Our Three Broken Relationships with God, Self, and Neighbor

God's Empowering Resources Cannot Flow In Broken & Uncaring Relationships & Human Dignity is Depleted

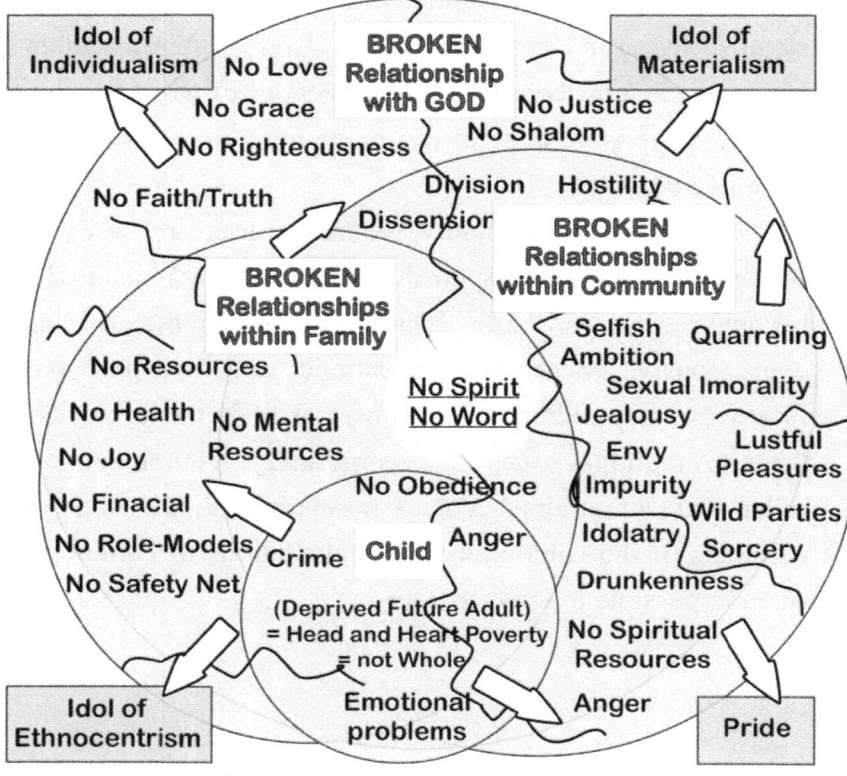

Idol of Individualism

BROKEN Relationship with GOD
- No Love
- No Grace
- No Justice
- No Shalom
- No Righteousness
- No Faith/Truth

Idol of Materialism

Division Hostility Dissension

BROKEN Relationships within Community
- Selfish Ambition
- Quarreling
- Sexual Immorality
- Jealousy
- Envy
- Lustful Pleasures
- Impurity
- Wild Parties
- Idolatry
- Sorcery
- Drunkenness
- No Spiritual Resources

BROKEN Relationships within Family
- No Resources
- No Health
- No Mental Resources
- No Joy
- No Financial
- No Role-Models
- No Safety Net
- Crime

No Spirit / No Word
No Obedience
Anger

Child (Deprived Future Adult) = Head and Heart Poverty = not Whole

Emotional problems

Anger

Idol of Ethnocentrism

Pride

And our culture wonders why we are so confused... fighting and arguing with each other while economic and spiritual poverty increases around us... and our children suffer from the lack of God's resource flow!

The Incarnational Community

When the foundations are being destroyed, what can the righteous do? (Psalm 11:3, NIV)

God our Father sent His Son into this fallen and broken world. Jesus, our model, moved into our lives in grace and truth. His incarnation (relocation) was not a short-term mission trip. He lived among us, as us: "The Word became flesh and made His dwelling among us. We have seen his glory, the glory of the one and only Son, who came from the Father, full of grace and truth" (John 1:14, NIV). He came to show us the Way, the Truth, and the Life (John 14:6). He is the Mediator of a New Covenant that releases believers from sin and empowers them by the Holy Spirit to know who they truly are and to be His many witnesses in our dark, fallen, and broken world. As he instructs his disciples in Acts 1:8a, "You will receive power when the Holy Spirit comes upon you; and you will be My witnesses" (NASB; see also John 16:7, 17:18). As noted in the *Life Application New Testament Commentary,* "This is an important and exciting theme in John's gospel. The Father sent the Son into the world, the Father and the Son sent the Spirit to the disciples, and the disciples are sent by the Father and Son into the world."[14]

In Christ, the new, true self has come, and the old, false self is gone (2 Corinthians 5:17). In Christ, we are freed and empowered to be loved and to love rightly. We are now Ambassadors and Bridge-Builders, representatives of Christ who

---

[14] Note on John 17:18, *Life Application New Testament Commentary* (Wheaton, IL: The Livingstone Corporation, 2001), 448.

reconcile all relationships with God and each other (2 Corinthians 5:20, NIV). Christ's Spirit and Word graciously enable and guide believers in faith, love, righteousness, and justice that restores shalom to the earth. And by redeeming a broken community, we find our own wholeness too—all for God's glory. According to the apostle Paul, God's intent in all of this "was that now through the Church, the manifold wisdom of God should be made known to the rulers and authorities in the heavenly realms, according to His eternal purpose which is accomplished in Christ Jesus our Lord" (Ephesians 3:10–11, NIV).

How can God's wisdom be made known to a broken world? Consider a Broken Community, where broken relationships abound, spiritual and economic poverty thrive, darkness and fallenness prevail, and a sense of hopelessness pervades the world. Then consider injecting even a small light of the "Beloved Whole Community" into this darkness. Consider how Jesus and His Spirit moved among us with grace and truth, releasing us from the darkness and developing and empowering us to see our true identity and live abundantly. The Church is now sent to do likewise according to the Word and Spirit of God in us. Thanks to God's grace, we are equipped with every spiritual gift needed for our mission (Ephesians 1:3).

The incarnational Church Body is to be the living proof of a loving God within a broken and dark world. For God's glory, the Church is to be the "light of the world" (Matthew 5:14), telling people who they truly are in Christ. **God the Father sent His Son; His Son sent His Spirit; the Spirit now sends His Church to be His Light in the darkness**—releasing and empowering those who are suffering and oppressed. In faithfully carrying our cross daily, we must also keep in mind the big picture given to us in the life, death, and resurrection of Jesus Christ. Suffering and death do not have the last word. In faithful love, there is always hope—a hope of resurrection on the far side of suffering.

Where are we to go? As Jesus' bias is toward the poor, so should our bias be. The generationally poor most clearly reflect the brokenness of our entire community. We are called to go to them as Jesus came to us.

What do we do? Relationally move into the lives of the poor and become friends, just as Christ became friends with us. Work to reconcile and redeem what has been lost of the Kingdom on earth.

As the following diagram depicts, when those who are centered in the Word and Spirit of Jesus move into the neighborhoods and lives of the poor, that very Word and Spirit then becomes the core of the heart and soul. From that core emanates the agape that will result in providing the transformation and many of the relational resources needed to move out of generational poverty.

Jesus loves you, frees you, and empowers you to love and become like Him.

"INCARNATIONAL COMMUNITY"

"The Word became flesh and made his dwelling among us." (John 1:14a, NIV)
"Jesus said,... As the Father has sent Me, I am sending you." (John 20:21, NIV)

3R's: RELOCATE- RECONCILE- REDEEM

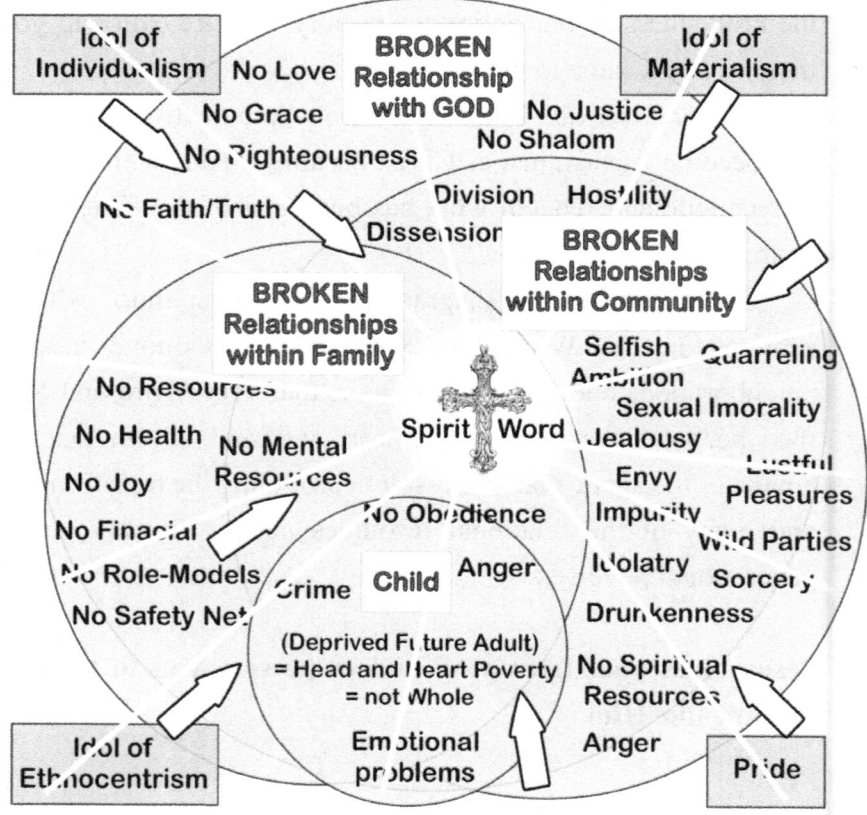

- **Idol of Individualism**
- **Idol of Materialism**
- **Idol of Ethnocentrism**
- **Pride**

BROKEN Relationship with GOD
- No Love
- No Grace
- No Justice
- No Shalom
- No Righteousness
- No Faith/Truth

BROKEN Relationships within Community
- Division
- Hostility
- Dissension
- Selfish Ambition
- Quarreling
- Sexual Imorality
- Jealousy
- Envy
- Lustful Pleasures
- Impurity
- Wild Parties
- Idolatry
- Sorcery
- Drunkenness

BROKEN Relationships within Family
- No Resources
- No Health
- No Joy
- No Mental Resources
- No Financial
- No Role-Models
- No Safety Net
- Crime

Child (Spirit / Word)
- No Obedience
- Anger
- (Deprived Future Adult)
- = Head and Heart Poverty
- = not Whole
- Emotional problems
- Anger
- No Spiritual Resources

"As Jesus moved into our lives, we are to move into the lives of others."

Becoming Whole People

The wholeness of the Kingdom of God is present where the King is present. The "Beloved Whole Community" is a theme throughout Scripture, although it is called by many names in many contexts. Paul calls this whole community the "Church" and the "Body of Christ." Genesis called it the "Garden of Eden" (Gen. 2:7–8). In Exodus, God called it "a priestly kingdom and a holy nation" (Ex. 19:3–6). Moses called it "a people of God's very own possession" (Deut. 4:12–20). The Psalmist called it "Zion," "the city of our God," and "the holy mountain" (Psalm 48:1,12–14). Isaiah called it "house of the God of Jacob," "Zion," and "Jerusalem" (Isa. 2:2–3). Zechariah called it "the holy mountain" (Zech. 8:3). John called it "the kingdom of our Lord and Messiah," "the holy city," and the "new Jerusalem" (Rev. 21:1–2). **Jesus called it "The Kingdom of God" (Lk. 17:20–21).** As Dr. Robert Linthicum points out, "Throughout the Bible these biblical leaders professed in common a single, clear-cut vision of God's intentions for the world."[15]

Thus, by becoming whole people who form whole communities, we are working to build God's Kingdom on earth and fulfill God's plan for mankind. To be whole, we must be *both* capable *and* caring. Often, we tend to fall short in one of these areas. This is why we must ask God to develop His character in us, for our own sake and for the sake of our community. We must submit to God's long-term plan of teaching, rebuking, correcting, and training (2 Timothy 3:16–17).

---

[15] Robert Linthicum, Building a People of Power: Equipping Churches to Transform Their Communities (Milton Keynes, UK: Authentic Media, 2005).

Meditate over the "Two Sides of the Whole Person" chart and ask God to reveal where He desires to make you whole:

TWO SIDES of the WHOLE PERSON		
CAPABLE + CARING = WHOLE PERSON		
"To acquire wisdom is to love oneself" (Proverbs 19:8, NLT)		
	CAPABLE SIDE	CARING SIDE
CONSCIOUS STRUGGLE	Mind Development, Right Thinking and Doing	Heart Development, Right Caring and Doing
VALUES	Truth (Sets free, "releases")	Love (Builds up, "develops")
GUIDE/ DISCERNMENT	Word Centered	Spirit Centered
PERSPECTIVE	Individual, Personal	Community, Social
VISION	Capable, Productive, Respected	Caring, Loving, Respecting
ROLE	Provide & Protect	Teach & Connect
SYNONYM	Economically Flush	Spiritually Flush
ANTONYM	Economically Poor. Doesn't know how to fish and becomes a burden.	Spiritually Poor. Doesn't care about the fishpond or fishermen.
GOSPEL PERSPECTIVE	"Love God" (Personal Gospel)	"Love your neighbor" (Social Gospel)
CRITIQUES OF THE OTHER SIDE	Love without Truth. (Soft, mushy, and needy without a developed mind)	Truth without Love. (Hard, critical, and greedy without a developed heart)
DEEPEST NEED	To Love & Respect	To Be Loved & Respected

Without "BOTH-AND" each side remains incomplete. To mature into Christlikeness requires us to enter our personal struggle to equally and actively allow God to develop BOTH OUR MINDS AND HEARTS for Wisdom's sake and God's glory.

"Conforming to the image of Jesus"

Internalizing the information in this diagram will help us to become people who make rational decisions. Extremely brilliant people often make irrational decisions. So do extremely caring folk. Why do capable people or caring people make bad decisions that cause harm? Albert Einstein rightly said that we cannot solve our problems with the same thinking we used when we caused them.[16] So what do we need to change about our thinking?

A whole person, as described in the diagram above, is able to make rational decisions. We generally make our decisions based on our dominant side of the whole person—our paradigm that causes us to fundamentally view the world either "as-it-is" or "as-it-should-be." Few have been trained to see and live out both sides simultaneously.

The pragmatic people who only see the world "as-it-is" make decisions and devise solutions with no vision of where they are going. In the here-and-now, they have no destination marked on the map. They think they know "here," but they have lost sight of "there"—of "on earth as it is in heaven."

The idealistic people who only see the world "as-it-should-be" have little understanding of themselves or what the world is truly like. They are typically seen as being naive and idealistic. They have a vision of "there," but they do not know "here." To get from "here" to "there," we need to truly know both the "here" and the "there" on the map of life as seen through God's eyes. The

---

[16] Debbie Woodbury, "My No. 1 Tip for Solving Problems," *Huffpost,* May 2, 2013, https://www.huffpost.com/entry/problem-solving-advice_b_3185536.

shortcomings of either pragmatism or idealism produce a bad witness for Christ.

To make proper choices, then, we need to see both where we are and where we want to go. Only then can we develop a plan to get "there." We can develop a vision of wholeness and strive to reach it: a vision of a "whole" society where people are no longer dependent upon government subsidies but are capable and caring people who can provide for themselves and their families and seek the well-being of their neighbors. It is certainly a tall order. But if the right plan is implemented, there is a real chance we can achieve it.

Justice and the Whole Community

All of this is not merely a scheme for us to achieve our own wholeness. This is a justice issue: we have to make things right. Scripture resounds with the theme of justice. In Amos 5:24 we read, "Let justice roll down like a river, righteousness like a never-failing stream!" (NIV). In Isaiah 61:8, God could not be clearer: "For I, the Lord, love justice" (NIV).

God obviously places a high value on justice in the Old Testament, but the word "justice" seems to all but disappear in the New Testament. It does not appear at all in some English translations of the New Testament. That could be a bit disconcerting for those who understand biblical justice to be central to Christianity. It is important to realize that in the New Testament, the Greek word *dikaiosune* is usually translated as "righteousness." But *dikaiosune,* in its broader sense, means both "righteousness" and "justice." God's heart for justice is so integrally linked to His righteousness that the same word is used in the New Testament to describe them. The word *dikaiosune* encompasses both of these characteristics of God and His Kingdom, but unfortunately, the English translators of the New Testament generally translate it only as "righteousness." This is despite the fact that the translators of classical Greek usually translate *dikaiosune* as justice (as in the *Iliad* and *Odyssey* by Homer). Unlike English, the Romance languages—Portuguese, Spanish, French, Latin, Italian, and Greek—all have one word for justice/righteousness, and the primary meaning is justice. So a reader of the New Testament in these languages will find "justice" much more often than a reader of English translations will.

Regardless of this peculiarity in translation, we must understand that God's justice and righteousness do not change between the Old and New Testaments. As to the Old Testament, Lowell Noble explains:

"Hebrews had a strong sense of community; a good Hebrew would understand that love requires one to do justice, but most American Christians (in general) do not grasp that Biblical love demands justice. Righteousness and justice were like Siamese twins in the Old Testament. A Hebrew could not claim to be personally righteous and neglect justice."[17]

In our New Testament English translations, we may gain a fuller understanding of biblical *dikaiosune* by reading "righteousness" as also denoting "justice." Developing this mental habit will open our minds and hearts to God's love for doing justice. Ultimately, though, it is our faith that ignites the grace of

---

[17] Lowell Noble, *From Oppression to Jubilee Justice* (Llumina Press, 2007), 82.

the Holy Spirit that empowers us to rightly love and do justice. As our faith expresses itself in love (Galatians 5:6), we are empowered by the Holy Spirit to seek righteousness and justice in harmony with the word of God. For in the end, love and justice are not opposed; rather, "Love is the soul of Justice."[18] And, conversely, "Justice is the framework for love."[19]

The last six of the Ten Commandments deal with justice. When Jesus was asked what the Greatest Commandment is, He taught us to love God and mankind wholeheartedly. But Jesus' Love Commandments were tightly connected to acting rightly and justly according to the Ten Commandments. According to Jesus, doing justice is doing love, and doing love is doing justice. Justice and love are tightly woven together in the King's Kingdom on earth.

What Causes Injustice?

Simply put, loving what God hates causes injustice. The root cause of injustice is man's displaced love for idols. Idolatry breaks relationships with God, self, and neighbors. It blinds us to God's truth, to the reality of Who He is and in Whose image we were originally created. In our fallen culture, we have normalized our idols to the point where we are unconscious of them and of their control over us. This anecdote from David Foster Wallace captures our condition:

---

[18] Latin American Bishops, *Mendellin Documents* (1968), Section 2.14.

[19] Fred Kammer, SJ, Doing Faithjustice: An Introduction to Catholic Social Thought (Matwah, NJ: Paulist Press, 2004), 194.

"There are two young fish swimming upstream and they happen to meet an older fish swimming the other way, who nods at them and says "Morning, boys. How's the water?" And the two young fish swim on for a bit, and then eventually one of them looks over at the other and says 'What the heck is water?'"[20]

Idolatry is the pink elephant in the room. We are unconscious of worshipping and following our idols. We say, "I do not have an idol!" even though we have chosen to believe that our culture is centered around "me" and my "group." We say, "I do not have an idol," while choosing to trust in the material things we possess. Like the stream the young fish swim in, idolatry is the cultural "water" we inhabit. Like the old fish, we must transcend our culture to see our idols. To become aware of our idolatry will require a renewing of our minds and a conscious choice to love what God tells us to love. If we do not do this work, our idols will consume us, individually and socially. Idolatry will break relationships and cause oppression, injustice, and poverty.

To understand justice, we need to understand oppression. To understand oppression, we need to understand idolatry. For it is our misplaced love for idols that breaks our relationships, oppresses others, and causes spiritual and economic poverty. When we succumb to idolatry, we choose to give place to our idols and addictions over God, self, neighbors, and even creation. Only in understanding the connection between idolatry, oppression, and injustice are we better able to understand justice

---

[20] David Foster Wallace, "2005 Kenyon Commencement Address," https://web.ics.purdue.edu/~drkelly/DFWKenyonAddress2005.pdf, 1.

and see its inseparable connection to the rightly ordered love our Lord commands.

Idol creation begins in small ways. Idolatry is usually a slow drift from good to bad to evil. Ironically, idolatry usually begins as the embrace of something good. God created everything and called it very good (Gen. 1:31, NIV: "God saw all that he had made, and it was very good"). Yet man will take what God created as good and make it evil when he begins to place creation above our Creator.

God is very serious about man's inclination toward idolatry. As such, the first two of His Ten Commandments concern idolatry:

You must not have any other god but me. You must not make for yourself an idol of any kind or an image of anything in the heavens or on the earth or in the sea. You must not bow down to them or worship them, for I, the Lord your God, am a jealous God who will not tolerate your affection for any other gods (Exodus 20:3–5, NLT).

In Mark 12:29, Jesus states the Jewish 'Shema' (Deuteronomy 6:4), "Hear, O Israel, the Lord our God, the Lord is one," and then joins it with His Greatest Commandments (Mark 12:30–31). These love directives guide mankind into the abundant life that our Father desires for us. They are also the antidote to our idolatrous tendencies. Loving what Christ Jesus tells us to love places us on the Kingdom Path, The Way to abundant life. To follow Jesus' greatest directives, His revealed Will, is for our own good and for the good of others. Our Father's great directives harmonize, unify, edify, identify and transform. People begin treating others the way they would like to be treated (Matthew 7:12; Luke 6:31).

To do God's Will honors the whole-istic process of developing His character in us. As the Spirit and Word develop Christ's character in us, we add faith and truth to God's grace; to that faith we add love; to love we add righteousness; and to righteousness we add justice. We join with others in right and just relationships that lead to shalom, peace, joy, and wholeness in the Kingdom of God on earth. As Jesus teaches us to pray, "Our Father...Thy Kingdom come, Thy Will be done on earth as it is in heaven" (Matthew 6:9–10).

> There are two sides to Justice:
> Release and Empower

The Two Sides of Justice

The biblical concept of justice is complex and ought to be further examined. How has God Himself done justice for His people? The Israelites were slaves in Egypt. God released them from their oppressions, brought them out of Egypt, and empowered them to become a self-sufficient people by giving them silver and gold and the Promised Land. They were both "released" and "empowered," just as we are in Christ. In the New Covenant, Jesus promises to both release believers from the oppressions of sin and empower them with His indwelling Spirit and His Law written on their newly transformed hearts of flesh.

God's two-sided approach of "Release" and "Empowerment" should be our model for justice. On the front side of the justice coin, a person is released from oppression. On the back side of the justice coin, a person is then empowered to become self-sufficient. The final goal of biblical justice is not merely to free people from oppression, but to grant them social and economic self-sufficiency that bring peace to society as a whole.

After a person is released from oppression, he or she needs to be relationally empowered to become both self-sufficient and caring—that is, to become a whole person. As our country has proceeded from the Agrarian Age into the Industrial Age and now into the Information Age, the empowerment gap among the generationally poor has become wider and wider. Human empowerment now requires more human development. The release side of the justice coin is often accomplished rather quickly, but the development-empowerment side of justice is usually a long-term endeavor and requires a person's character, work ethic, morals, education, job skills, and workplace, and social etiquette, etc. to be developed. A multifaceted approach is necessary, for there is no silver bullet or quick fix to achieve human development and empowerment. Doing love and justice will take a lot of time and commitment and will be expensive.

Historically, justice has usually only been done halfway. In America, we often work for release, but we rarely develop or empower. Thus, the old injustice only morphs into a subtler new oppression. For example, slaves were released from their bondage of slavery into an agrarian culture, but not empowered with forty acres and a mule (which they had earned) to become self-sufficient. At that point in America, there was less development needed, as the freed slaves knew how to farm. They only needed to be empowered with land. But because this empowerment did not occur, the old oppression of slavery quickly morphed into the harder-to-see injustice of the Jim Crow laws. As the American economy grew and developed over time, the empowerment gap grew too. One hundred years later, the Civil Rights movement again "released" people from the injustices of Jim Crow, but the "development" and "empowerment" side of justice was not done. Jim Crow only morphed into the entitlements programs that generationally trap a large percentage of Black Americans. The lesson of our history is that to avoid immoral and oppressive systems both sides of justice need to be done for there to be peace, wholeness, and shalom.

On the liberal side of Christianity, people who cannot stand oppression say their goal is to release people from oppression. On the conservative side of Christianity, oppression is to be solved by providing self-sustaining jobs. But when either side is asked to hire the generationally poor, their response is, "We can't hire the generationally poor because they have no education, no training, no work ethic; they have no soft social skills to hold a job; many cannot pass a drug test; and many cannot pass the physical. Heck, they do not even know how to rightly think, care, or act! We can't hire the generationally poor!" This is evidence of the growing "empowerment gap" between liberation and jobs. Biblical justice demands that Christians faithfully enter this growing empowerment gap for the sake of the dignity of all people.

Why Are So Many Christians Blind to the Empowerment Gap?

There are at least two reasons why Christians do not realize the need to develop and empower the poor:

1) No vision of the back side of the Justice Coin. Without this vision, there can be no intentional mission to enter and bridge the gap formed by injustice.
2) Idols. Idolatrous folk just don't care about justice for others. They cannot see or hear the cries of the oppressed. They willingly ignore their neighbors and blame others. Society's problems are rooted in people not caring about what God cares about.

Based on these reasons, failing to address the development and empowerment side of justice is both a "vision" and "heart" issue. If we do not develop a vision of empowerment and allow our hearts to be changed by the word and Holy Spirit, the empowerment gap will not only remain but continue to grow. This is a tragedy, for all people deeply desire to be loved and to love, to be free, and to have the power to become whole. They long for an abundant life where nothing is broken and nothing is lost. In other words, whether they know it or not, they long for the Shalom of the Kingdom of God. But Shalom can never be present where idolatry and injustice prospers.

The Vision of Shalom

"Love and faithfulness meet together; righteousness and peace [shalom] kiss each other. Faithfulness springs forth from the earth, and righteousness looks down from heaven." (Psalm 85:10–11, NIV)

"Peacemakers who sow in peace raise a harvest of righteousness." (James 3:18, NIV)

"Blessed [spiritually calm with life-joy in God's favor] are the makers and maintainers of peace, for they will [express His character and] be called the sons of God." (Matthew 5:9, AMP)

The noun *shalom* means peace, wellness, health, or prosperity. It is the verb form *shalam*, though, that provides a deeper understanding of this term as it is used in theology, doctrine, and liturgy. Literally translated, *shalam* means to bring to a place of safety, but figuratively it points to completeness. In its use in Scripture, shalom describes the actions that lead to a state of wholeness. Shalom seems not to merely speak of a state of affairs, but describes a Shalom Process, an activity, a movement towards fullness.

The use of *shalom* in the Scriptures always points to a transcendent movement toward wholeness. Shalom is used in reference to the wellbeing of others (Genesis 43:27, Exodus 4:18) and in prayer for the wellbeing of cities or nations (Psalm 122:6, Jeremiah 29:7). Yet its transcendence lies in its inseparable relationship to grace, faithfulness, truth, love, righteousness, and justice (2 Peter 1:2; Psalm 85:10; Isaiah 9:7; 48:18, 22; 54:10; 57:19–21; 2 Corinthians 13:11; Galatians 5:22–23). The hope of shalom inspires the prophecies about the work of the coming Messiah. These prophecies refer to the Messiah's revelation as the time of peace (Haggai 2:7–9; Isaiah 2:2–4; 11:1–9) and even grant this anointed one the title "Prince of Peace" (Isaiah 9:6; Micah 5:4–5a). God's anointed will be the Prince of Shalom.

In the Christian Scriptures, the Greek term *eirene* means peace. Like its Hebrew counterpart, it has connotations of transcendence. Its meaning is best understood in relation to terms like grace (Romans 1:7), righteousness (Romans 14:17), and life (Romans 8:6). The word is also employed in benedictions, like those in 1 Thessalonians 5:23 and Hebrews 13:20–21, perhaps echoing the prayers of peace common throughout the Hebrew Scriptures and Jewish benedictions (see Numbers 6:22–27).

The sense of completeness central to the term *shalom* can also be confirmed in homophonic terms found in other Semitic languages. The term *shelam*, of Chaldean origin, seems to mean both "peace" and "restoration." Aramaic derivations of the terms *shalom* and *shalam* are said to refer to peace, safety, completeness, and welfare. The Assyrian term *salamu* means to be complete, unharmed, and paid/atoned. *Sulmu*, another Assyrian term, means welfare. Also related to *shalom* is the Arabic root *salaam*, meaning to be safe, secure, and forgiven, among other things. The word also contains the idea of a personal commitment to peace: *salaam* is the root for the terms Muslim and Islam, which are literally translated "he or she who submits to God" and "submission to God," respectively.

Shalom is the King's Kingdom vision—a vision of an earth where nothing is broken and nothing is lost, a place where there are no burdens and no gaps. There is a sense of safety and security; all people are capable and caring; all life has meaning, purpose, and dignity. It is a place where there is peace with God, peace with self, peace with neighbors, and peace with all creation. It is a place where whole, capable, and caring people make up whole families, whole neighborhoods, whole communities; a place joyfully unified and centered in Christ Jesus and characterized by God's grace, faith, truth, love, righteousness, and justice. This shalom vision is our picture of the Kingdom "on earth as it is in heaven," of the creation restored to its original good purpose bestowed by the Creator. A Kingdom on earth where social capital, economic capital, educational capital, emotional capital, physical capital, and in all spiritual capital lovingly and justly flow throughout our community and into the lives of all families and children.

Strengthening Social Capital

Robert Putnam's bestseller, "Bowling Alone: The Collapse and Revival of American Community" popularized the term "Social Capital". Putnam argued that while Americans have become wealthier their sense of community has withered. Cities and traditional suburbs have given way to "edge cities" and "exurbs" – vast, anonymous places where people sleep and work and do little else. As people spend more and more time in the office, commuting to work and watching TV alone, there's less time for joining community groups and voluntary organizations, and socializing with neighbors, friends and even family. To demonstrate this decline, Putnam looked at the way Americans play 10-pin bowling, a sport with a big following in the United States. He found that although bowling has never been bigger, Americans are no longer competing against each other in the once-popular local leagues. Instead, they are – literally – bowling alone.

Putnam argued that the decline of the community networks that once led Americans to bowl together represents a loss of social capital."[21]

Intentionally strengthening a community's Social Capital is key to releasing its economic capital, educational capital, emotional capital, physical capital and of course its spiritual capital. 'Capital' is a broad term that can describe anything that confers value or benefit to its owners. These six capital resources are assets or values that add to the long-term wholeness, peace and joy of community life. The extent to which we acquire these six capital resources reflects a specific poverty or richness in our lives. That is, a person can be rich spiritually, but poor economically. A person can be rich economically, but poor spiritually. But in right and caring relationships these six capital resources together can develop a more whole individual and community.

Social Capital reflects mutually respectful relationships, friendships, families, community connectedness, shared values, and trustworthiness among people. Social capital represents relational networks and engaged involvement among people.

One of Putnam's points is that community connectedness is not just about warm fuzzy tales of civic triumph. In measurable and well-documented ways, social capital makes an enormous difference in our lives...Social capital makes us smarter, healthier, safer, richer, and better able to govern a just and stable democracy.

Putnam also put forth the argument that school performance,

---

[21] Simon and Schuster Paperbacks, Rockefeller Center, 1230 Avenue of the Americas N.Y., N.Y. 10020, copyright 2000.

public health, crime rates, clinical depression, tax compliance, philanthropy, race relations, community development, census returns, teen suicide, economic productivity, campaign finance, even simple human happiness - all are demonstrably affected by how (and whether) we connect with our family and friends and neighbors and co-workers.

Social Capital takes many different forms in all our social relationships and networks. It can be a friend that does home maintenance for the elderly. Social capital can be a school teacher who also coaches basketball, or volunteers who come together each year to organize an event for a charity. Social Capital is our community's "glue" and "WD-40", where love holds it all together and trust allows for smooth transactions. It can be a bowling league or neighborhood association or community club. Social Capital can be experienced in a Church's discipling programs for their children's educational and training programs. Social Capital is a matter of shared values, trusting relationships and resulting friendships. It can be experienced in a Church's outreach. It can be experienced as a process of steps like Alcoholic Anonymous' 12-Step Programs that meet regularly all over town. This mobilization of people can be experienced in business and government where there are shared goals, values and trust too. Wherever you find people coming together, building trusting relationships, or networking to get things done, you will see social capital at work improving your community.

There are two different types of Social Capital: Bonding Social Capital and Bridging Social Capital. Bonding Social Capital happens naturally. It represents networks of people coming together who are alike. This Bonding Social Capital is represented by the saying "birds of a feather flock together".

Bridging Social Capital does not happen naturally and must be an intentional action. It represents networks of people coming together who are not alike. This Bridging Social Capital is represented and defined in scripture as loving our neighbor (who Jesus described as not being like us).

Bonding Social Capital is a good thing, unless it is done without Bridging Social Capital. If Bonding Capital is left alone, our ingrown ethnocentric thinking begins to take root where we say, "we are 'in', they are 'out'" ... "we are 'right' and they are 'wrong'." Bonding Social Capital must always be intentionally balanced with Bridging Social Capital for our individual and community's wholeness sake.

COMMUNITY: Social Capital is about building and strengthening CommUnity. "Community isn't just a function of abstract relationships. Community is experienced in space and time. True community happens when a small enough group of people share a small enough amount of space and a large enough amount of time to make a serious difference in each other's lives. To learn to love one another face to face in practical and necessary ways. Any quest for building community that doesn't also take space and time seriously will be artificial and, finally, frustrating." (Quote by Ken Myers).

Community' has it's root meaning in "common unity". Common unity reflects shared values, trusting and loving relationships with God, others and self(s).

In scripture God's community is described as the Kingdom of God which we are to seek first and foremost. It is this community goal and Christlike character that human beings are designed for and deeply yearn for.

Matthew 6:33 (Amp), "But first and most importantly se (aim at, strive after) His kingdom and His righteousness [His way of doing and being right—the attitude and character of God], and all these things will be given to you also."

Our scriptural pathway to acquiring this Kingdom community of high social capital and mutually benefitting networks is the way of love and given to us in Jesus' Greatest Commandments that all the Law and the Prophets are based, depend on and hang from. The Greatest Commandments direct us towards living in right and caring relationships with God, neighbors, and selves. In these right and caring relationships, social capital and community are strengthened through the flow of the six capital resources. (Note: There will be many surprising and unforeseen resources that begin to flow).

The Guiding Rules of strengthening Social Capital are given to us in Jesus' Greatest Commandments:

Matthew 22:37-40 (NLT), Jesus replied, "'You must love the Lord your God with all your heart, all your soul, and all your mind. 38 This is the first and greatest commandment. 39 A second is equally important: 'Love your neighbor (i.e., Bridging Social Capital) as yourself (i.e., Bonding Social Capital).' 40 The entire law and all the demands of the prophets are based on these two commandments."

And we are promised in Deut. 15:4 & 5 (NLT) that **"There should be no poor among you,** for the Lord your God will greatly bless you in the land he is giving you as a special possession. 5 You will receive this blessing **IF you are careful to obey all the commands of the Lord your God ...."**

CHAPTER 5

NEXT STEPS

First let us summarize where we have been. As God's beloved agents here on earth, we are called to love God and to bring Him glory. He makes it clear that our love for Him is demonstrated when we keep His commandments (John 14:15). The greatest of these is to love Him wholeheartedly and to love our neighbor as ourselves. We are to recognize our idols and remove them from our hearts because they cause oppression, which results in injustice and poverty. We will be unable to truly and properly love our neighbor until we see them and ourselves, not as the world does, but as God does, with love, truth, and dignity. He sees us as His children (John 1:12); His friends (John 15:15); a new creation (2 Cor. 5:17); chosen, holy, blameless (Eph. 1:4); a temple of the Holy Spirit (1 Cor. 3:16); righteous and holy (Eph. 4:24, 2 Cor. 5:21); and so much more. God desires us to be filled with grace for our neighbor and to provide mercy where it is needed, but to provide tough-love where it is warranted as well. As this development process helps a person stand on his own two feet, his or her God-given dignity is restored. This is God's will for all of us, since we are created in His image (Gen. 1:27).

For purposes of this book, we, as Christ followers, ought to see ourselves as Paul does in Ephesians 2:10: "For we are God's masterpiece. He has created us anew in Christ Jesus, so we can do the good things he planned for us long ago" (NLT). All God intends for us to do (those good works He prepared in advance) is a function of obeying the Greatest Commandment. As we spend time in the Word and Holy Spirit, our hearts and minds are renewed (Ro. 12:2), and our love for and desire to please God grows. When we put Him first, we become more mindful that our many idols can supplant Him at any given moment. We recognize that He is both Savior and Lord and that as His servants we are in submission to His will. The sacrificial agape love He desires us to have is impossible to develop in our own strength, but if we are willing to let the Holy Spirit demonstrate love like this through us, it will be done.

We are called to not only love God, but to glorify Him too. How do we glorify our Lord? Romans 8:28–30 tells us that "in all things God works for the good of those who love him, who have been called according to his purpose. For those God foreknew he also predestined to be conformed to the image of his Son....And those he predestined, he also called; those he called, he also justified; those he justified, he also glorified" (NIV). Thus, "those who love Him, who have been called according to His purpose" are predestined to be glorified in the image of our Savior and Lord in our daily lives.

Putting aside our idols allows us to work against the oppression of others that we witness and, in some instances, may even create. Those in the middle class, which probably describes many of our readers, are typically capable. They have regular jobs; they have families, friendships, in some cases mentors. But they may be weak when it comes to caring about the well-being of others (especially those unlike themselves). We need to realize the areas where we are poor in love and generosity towards our neighbors, even if we are comfortably well-off from a material standpoint. If we hope to "walk" with an under-resourced person and help him become whole, we need to become whole ourselves.

As we properly see and love ourselves and love our neighbor accordingly, we begin to see God's Kingdom realized on earth "as it is in heaven." The result is the restoration of God-given dignity, the end of individualism, materialism, and racism, and communities of whole people where God's love and justice prevail for all. In loving God, neighbor and self we begin to strengthen our social capital that releases our financial capital, educational capital, emotional capital, physical capital and spiritual capital into our community.

Establishing a Vision

Being created in the image and likeness of God, mankind deeply desires to live in the Kingdom of God where wholeness, peace, and joy reign. Yet our deep desires are thwarted by the reality of the world's brokenness (i.e., "sexual immorality, impurity and debauchery; idolatry/gods and spiritual witchcraft; hatred, discord, jealousy, fits of rage, selfish ambition, dissensions, factions and envy; drunkenness, orgies, and the like" [Gal 5:19–21]). To develop a pathway, a mission, we must first have a biblically rooted vision of what God desires us to become while also having a realistic understanding of where we are now. We then need a missional pathway that connects our realistic assessment of who we are to our ideal of who God wants us to become, both individually and collectively. This missional pathway will not come from the level upon which our issues were created, but from the highest level of God's own commands. Thus, the from-here-to-there process of Kingdom building must begin and end with the Body of Christ in our local community.

America has become a country of -holics. We have chosen to place our faith in everything but the truth of our Savior and Lord. Our disordered objects of love (i.e., idols) break relationships, oppress, and unjustly create poverty in our minds, hearts, bodies, families, neighborhoods, communities, states, and nation. Our idols cannot deliver what they promise. They keep us from taking responsibility for our behaviors and attitudes and lead us to criticize and blame others. We argue and point fingers, trying to cast blame on anything but ourselves. We point at Politics/Government/Welfare, Jobs/Businesses, in-grown Churches, Education/Schools/Teachers, Families/Neighborhoods, Ethnocentrism/Racism, etc. We cannot seem to come together as a people, for our misplaced loves continually divide us. How are we to come together and move forward as one?

Unity has to begin with God renewing our minds and transforming our hearts. It has to begin with the family of God centering itself in both Christ's Spirit and Word. And then we who are transformed must be Christ's Ambassadors of Reconciliation. Paul lays out this vision for God's people and the world in 2 Corinthians 5:17–20 (NIV):

"Therefore, if anyone is in Christ, the new creation has come: The old has gone, the new is here! All this is from God, who reconciled us to himself through Christ and gave us the ministry of reconciliation: that God was reconciling the world to himself in Christ, not counting people's sins against them. And he has committed to us the message of reconciliation. We are therefore Christ's ambassadors, as though God were making his appeal through us."

Elsewhere, Paul says that God is building a house "with Christ Jesus Himself as the chief cornerstone. In Him the whole building is joined together and rises to become a holy temple in the Lord" (Eph. 2:20–21, NIV). God is building His Beloved Community, the Church, so that "now, through the church, the manifold wisdom of God should be made known" (Eph. 3:10). The Church is called by God to be His presence on the earth, to bring humanity into relationship with Him and each other.

Common Groan

What is it that you hate seeing in this world? What is your Holy Discontent, your groan?

People and their systems will mobilize around their common groan, especially if it is a Holy Groan. What is your community or state's common groan? Do you groan because your state (city, community) is ranked low in economic growth or education, health, or childhood well-being? Or because it is ranked high in crime, childhood death, or illiteracy? Do we groan for our state, our city, our families, and our children? Or do we choose to ignore the reality of the poverty that surrounds us and is in us?

In our unending Blame Game, there is one person who is blameless. It is the generationally poor child. This child did not choose to be born in extreme brokenness, marginalization, and poverty. Yet it is this child that Jesus places among us and says,

"Behold, this child holds the keys to the Kingdom of God." Yes, this most vulnerable child holds the keys to our wholeness, individually and collectively. For this child is truly the least among us! It is this blameless generationally under-resourced child, our common groan, that we as a community can mobilize around and intentionally build up. By helping this child, we can become whole.

Can we envision systems that resource, develop, and empower the generationally poor child in the context strengthening social capital? Can we envision building relational "bridges" to this child ourselves? Can our collective groan for the under-resourced child motivate us into unified action to preserve and restore human dignity? The work will be difficult, but once we have a vision, it is possible.

So, How Is This to Be Done?

Hopefully, you have been impacted on a heart level and not merely a head level. If so, let the word and Holy Spirit have His way in you. If you are disturbed or upset by the plight of those in generational poverty (especially our generationally under-resourced children), consider taking action. Talk to your church. Look around your community and see where God is at work building bridges of truth and love. There are likely a dozen Christian non-profits that are assisting and developing people in poverty in your area. They usually deal with either "relief," "rehab," or "development." Remember that relief (feeding fish to the hungry) should be short term, while development (teaching them to fish) is long-term and often more relational. Seek out these ministries and take a plunge. Ask how you can help serve – typically this will be by either volunteering, investing and or praying. After you take action, reflect and meditate before acting again. Allow the cycles of your actions and reflections to drill you deeper into relationship with your neighbor and Lord. Along your journey, continuously allow God's indwelling Spirit and Word to teach and guide you. Allow His Spirit and word in you to destroy your idols and transform you. If God has put a specific burden and plan of action on your heart, see how it can be implemented alongside what already exists. Remember that whatever we do, if it does not begin and end in love, we are simply wasting our time. Jesus directs us in His Greatest Commandment to love God, self, and neighbor with all our mind, heart, and strength. This requires a walk of faith that turns on the Holy Spirit and conforms us to the image of Jesus. This is the Agape Way to the Kingdom. Only in the presence of right and caring relationships do spiritual, educational, emotional, social, economic, physical, financial, and relational resources flow for the edification of the under-resourced child, family, neighborhood, and us. It is only when we obey the Greatest Commandments that "there shall be no poor among you" (Deut. 15:4).

Learning to Love

Christians know that we are called to know God, love God, and glorify God, and that to love God is to obey His commands (1 John 5:3). We know we are to love our neighbor. But how? We may theoretically grasp these things, but if we do not know God, we cannot love Him. If we do not know our neighbors, we cannot love them. If we try to love without knowing, we will cause harm. How then are we to have a personal and loving relationship with both God and neighbor? At Bridge Ministry of Acadiana, we have learned to love God by loving our neighbor who is not like us. We have learned to love our neighbors by first loving their children, especially those who are generationally under-resourced.

Three R's of Christian Development

Where do we begin? To help us develop a deeper personal relationship with both God and neighbor, Dr. John Perkins developed Christian Community Development Association's Three R's of Christian Development: 1) Relocation, 2) Reconciliation, and 3) Redemption.

Relocation

Jesus Christ relocated to us, because the best way to serve is by being in close personal relationship to those being served. As Jesus moves into our neighborhood, we are to go and do the same. At Bridge, we have humbly relocated into a specific under-resourced inner-city neighborhood with the intention of becoming friends with our neighbors who live there.

Reconciliation

We understand that the root cause of poverty is man's broken relationships with God, self, and neighbors. We also know that we are called to be Christ's Ambassadors of reconciliation (2

Cor. 5:18–20). In reconciled relationships, resources will rightly flow to our under-resourced neighbors and their children. Reconciliation is best done among those in our closest proximity, in the context of personal relationships with both God and neighbor.

Redemption

Christ's indwelling Spirit and Word graciously enable and guide believers in faith, truth, love, righteousness, and justice to redeem what has been broken and lost of God's Kingdom on earth. Just as Christ demonstrated agape love to us by paying the ultimate price, we are to pay the same price in love in order to bring wholeness, peace, and joy to entire communities. In redeeming the wholeness of *this* under-resourced neighborhood, we find our wholeness too, both as individuals and communities.

When alleviating poverty through human development there seem to be two schools of thought: 1) those focused on Personal Responsibility, and 2) those focused on Social Responsibility. Much like our Personal Gospel to love God, and our Social Gospel to love our neighbors, the focus should be on a 'both-and' formula, not a one-sided 'either-or' formula. Most conservative Christians embrace the personal gospel, while liberal Christians embrace the social gospel. Human development and empowerment requires the wise and respectful embrace of both.

The Social Responsibility Question: How can we and our community wisely take *social responsibility* for our empowerment and the empowerment of our generationally under-resourced neighbors without causing the distortion of human dignity and further harm?

The Personal Responsibility Question: How can we and our community wisely encourage ourselves and our under-resourced neighbors to take *person*al *respon*sibility for the empowerment of our neighbors lives without causing the distortion of human dignity and further harm?

Our Three Major Delivery Systems

Social, economic, mental, emotional, physical and spiritual development of the generationally under-resourced neighborhood/family/child is critical to human wellness. Our nation has three major delivery systems: 1) Church, 2) Business, and 3) Government Systems. These delivery systems are designed to deliver unique resources to the community they serve, and thus each one has a role to play in poverty alleviation. As to the church, every major religion has as one of its principal tenets helping the needy. The Judeo-Christian culture on which this nation was founded strongly emphasizes this moral duty (although not perfected or fulfilled). Yet for generations, the highly resourced churches do not know the economically poor and thus remain spiritually poor. In the business realm, tackling the root causes of the problem of generational poverty will require acknowledging our idols, opening opportunities to meet the poor, form relational and development networks, job training and jobs. Many adults who are economically stuck in generational poverty have never held a job, nor do they have any family members who have ever worked. This lack of a model makes it difficult for the under-resourced to even conceive of working at a regular job. The multifaceted resources and time necessary to empower an under-resourced child is where business can play a major role. Finally, the government can fill in the gaps left by church and business, for example by providing financial resources to the most destitute. Equally important, though, is the government's ability to establish laws, influence and disseminate information that will enable and motivate systems to work together to combat generational poverty.

However, since there has been no unifying vision shared by these three institutions, they often do not work in unity with each other. We need to take a deeper look at how we can effectively and efficiently mobilize the many diverse resources from our three delivery systems around our community's common groan, our generationally under-resourced child and grow with them.

In poverty alleviation we must always remember God's view of us in Revelation 3:17 (NLT), "You say, 'I am rich. I have everything I want. I don't need a thing!' And you don't realize that you are wretched and miserable and poor and blind and naked." Let us remember that we are all poor in God's holistic view of poverty, but He promises us that by wholeheartedly loving God, self(s) and neighbors we will all become whole.

We can see the indications of many broken relationships in the economically impoverished child by measuring their Achievement Gap. For generations, the under-resourced child has arrived at school 1–2 years behind other children. This Achievement Gap has been ever widening. To close this Achievement Gap may require Extended Day Schools (two to three hours added to the end of the regular school day for homework assistance and tutoring) and Extended Year Schools (typically a six-week summer camp that combines school with fun in order to prevent the child from losing what they learned by the time the following school year rolls around). These programs provide education, life skills, and character development, but they require significant investment from the surrounding community. To satisfy our common groan will require the further injection of development-based (not relief-based) resources from our churches, government, and businesses working together in the lives of our community's generationally under-resourced children.

It may be noted that the Achievement Gap measured in our under-resourced children grows into the Development Gap when they are teens and then grows into their Empowerment Gap when they are adults. This empowerment gap is the gap between an unaware, uneducated or untrained adult and their ability to attain self-sufficiency. This is why God-given dignity can become unrecognizable and why justice must end in economics.

The Old Testament is filled with admonitions by God to give a hand-up to the poor and the oppressed, the widows, the fatherless, and the aliens. This concept, to help the needy, is stated repeatedly in both the Old and New Testaments and is clearly a high priority for God. This makes sense given the Greatest Commandments: first, to love God above all else, and second, to love your neighbor as you love yourself. When asked in response to these commandments, "Who is my neighbor?" Jesus responds with the story of the Good Samaritan— a people despised by the Jews. Thus, the charge to Christians is to love even those we may not like and who are unlike us.

At present, all across the country there are various nonprofits that do wonderful work with the economically poor and in the inner cities. But there is room for many more such ministries. Since churches are uniquely designed to be highly relational, it is important for them to consider starting their own nonprofit or perhaps joining with other churches to do so. Anyone who has volunteered at a church-led nonprofit has seen members of the congregation being drawn closer to God and to each other and, crucially, to the poor in their cities and towns. What better place to motivate the middle class to get involved than through extending their church families to an under-resourced family and neighborhood? This is not meant to denigrate the wonderful work of so many secular nonprofits but to point out the fact that a true Christian is in a better position to get involved, go beyond conventional charity, and extend the loving family of God to under-resourced families and their children. Christians who keep the Greatest Commandments in mind know that our loving actions must end in loving friendships, or we are 'clanging cymbals'.

Many white people are burdened by guilt about the way black people have been treated. John Perkins speaks of this in *A Quiet Revolution*:

"What we need are Christians who can get beyond their guilt and so get beyond light charity and really get involved in the black and poor community. I personally believe that it is only the supernatural power of God's forgiveness that can deal with personal guilt and put it behind you.

...If white and black people could yoke up together that way, some real burdens could be moved. That's my hope.

This hope— founded on forgiveness and reconciliation— demands some deep changes in values and requires us to allow God to deal with us as people in ways that are almost unheard of in our society.

White people must allow the gospel to penetrate their culture. Whites must allow the gospel to speak deeply to their broken, exploitative, superior, unjust lifestyles and attitudes. White Christians who claim Christ as Savior must also make Him Lord over such areas as spending, racial attitudes, and business dealings. Whites must see that the oppression of black people in this country runs deep throughout both our cultures. And anything short of a fundamental change of values (which we believe possible only through a relationship with Jesus Christ) will result in viewing the problem as "the black problem" and offering solutions like charity and welfare which have within them the same seeds of destructive exploitation and dehumanizing greed that oppresses the poor in the first place.

Black people must allow the gospel to penetrate their culture. Integration, equal opportunity, welfare, charity, and all these programs fail to deal with the deep-seated values that cause the bankruptcy in our black communities. These programs only serve to conform people to this world. Only the gospel can transform people by the renewing of their minds (Ro. 12:2).

The problems we face are primarily problems of values, not structures. It is not reform we need, but revolution, a whole new thing. The old needs to be passed away and the new ushered in. We cannot afford to easily condemn the white person by judging his past or simply condone the black person by understanding his past. We must call each other to be transformed."[22]

What we value and love the most, we ultimately become. If we value and love money the most, we become centered in material things. If we love our group or race the most, then we become ethnocentric and centered in our group first and foremost. If we love alcohol the most, we become alcoholics and centered

---

[22] John Perkins, *A Quiet Revolution*, 194, 197.

in self. These are a few of the idols/gods that represent America's Unholy Trinity and are idols that we will do whatever it takes to acquire and hold on to with a death grip. Idols are sins that divide, oppress, and create injustice and poverty .... And because we are a culture of "holics" and "isms" we unknowingly create social systems that perpetuate division, oppression, injustice, and poverty. This is why many liberal Christians call out for "social justice" to the conservative Christian's dismay. **The Bible speaks of idols/gods more than any other issue for a reason, yet idolatry is interestingly spoken of the least from our pulpits (for a reason as well).** Fact is the Church is the only system of the three delivery systems that is equipped to address idolatry and their root cause of broken relationships and poverty.

So, the basis of creating a transforming environment is to be centered in Christ in both Word and Spirit. We need transformed people who are willing to commit for a long period of time and become friends around their common groans regardless of the lack of immediate, positive results. This transforming environment is best found in the Christian community. Further, extended church families provide a readily available source of volunteers that need to learn how to meet and actively love their neighbors without causing further harm while maturing in their own faith. When these family-extending volunteers form genuine cross-cultural friendships, transformation of both results and idols die. If even 50% of adults in this country are churchgoers, and if 1% of this 50% become willing volunteers, then this would involve over 1,000,000 people that are learning to grow their hearts.

Another reason to focus on the churches is that the only way to have any real success with the poor is if the work is humbly done out of knowledge and love for God and the friend in need.

Many of the poor are not even aware of the need for and the blessings that come with growing, nurturing, and loving relationships. Not until the materially rich and poor meet do they both realize their true temporal and eternal need for each other (Luke 16:19-31).

Various development nonprofits maintain different focuses, employ different approaches, and reach different groups. But each is attempting to empower the poor with one or more resources. There are any number of ways that churches and nonprofits can make a difference in the lives of the generationally poor. Many under-resourced children, through no fault of their own, find themselves 1–2 years behind in school by fourth grade. This number is based on NAEP reports associated with Free and Reduced lunch recipients and the size of the Achievement Gap their test scores indicate.[23] In many instances, under-resourced children suffer from Adverse Childhood Experiences (A.C.E.s) and the poverty they find themselves in is not just economic but also social, emotional, physical, mental, and spiritual. Thus, the aim of a holistic after-school and summer school enrichment program is to create relational community networks that deliver and develop these resources in the child.

---

[23] See "ACEs and Toxic Stress: Frequently Asked Questions," published by Harvard University's Center on the Developing Child (https://developingchild.harvard.edu/resources/aces-and-toxic-stress-frequently-asked-questions/), and Mark Dynarski and Kirsten Kainz, "Why federal spending on disadvantaged students (Title I) doesn't work," Brookings Institute, November 20, 2015, https://www.brookings.edu/research/why-federal-spending-on-disadvantaged-students-title-i-doesnt-work/.

For most of the kids, the "Summer Slide" is particularly troublesome, making it necessary to use valuable school time in the new year to relearn things forgotten over the summer. A "summer learning experience" that is both fun and mentally challenging can keep them in the game over the summer break. What would such a program require?

Out of churches can come teachers, mentors, and volunteers, as well as financial contributions and prayers. But such a program should not *only* involve the church. To satisfy our common groan additional resources and networks must be provided by other sources. From the government can come the public school building where such a program can be conducted along with a hot meal in the afternoon for each child. If a high poverty religious school participates, then it is the government that can provide those students with vouchers and tuition tax credit scholarships to cover the cost of attending that school of their choice.

And let's not overlook business. In closing the achievement, development, and empowerment gaps of the poor child local businesses can regularly share resources with these programs, along with providing needed income, materials, job shadowing, and career teaching. Many finance field trips, and many of the business owners and their employees actually make charitable contributions; contribute to tuition tax credit scholarships that flow to the lower-income families.

This community type school that extends the family's resources is just one example of our three delivery systems' partnerships in helping to break the cycles of poverty. Not by doing "for", but "with" and "together".

It appears that those in government had good intentions when they developed various programs on both the federal and state levels through which the poor could receive money. But unintended consequences have worked the opposite effect, creating dependence instead of prosperity. Star Parker, an African-American columnist, writes on this issue:

"Six years ago I wrote a book called "Uncle Sam's Plantation." I wrote the book to tell my own story of what I saw living inside the welfare state and my own transformation out of it.

I said in that book that indeed there are two Americas. A poor America on socialism and a wealthy America on capitalism.

... A vast sea of well-intentioned government programs, all initially set into motion in the 1960s, that were going to lift the nation's poor out of poverty.

Instead of solving economic problems, the government welfare socialism created monstrous moral and spiritual problems. The kind of problems that are inevitable when individuals turn responsibility for their lives over to others.

Through God's grace, I found my way out. It was then that I understood what freedom meant and how great this country is."[24]

Due to America' Holy Trinity there are historic systems in housing, education, marginalization, employment, family, neighborhoods, etc. that hold people in poverty for generations, while often times benefitting corporations and the economically rich. These perpetuating systems are often reinforced by government, business, and churches and are perfectly designed to

---

[24] Star Parker, "Back on Uncle Sam's Plantation," *Townhall,* February 9, 2009, https://townhall.com/columnists/starparker/2009/02/09/back-on-uncle-sams-plantation-n1009056.

produce the product they produce. For example, reliance on subsidies from the government does not create freedom but puts people deeper into dependency and creates false markets in business.

Human beings have an innate desire for liberty, and a strong need to be empowered to earn what they get. To hand out money decade after decade has diminished and will continue to diminish this dignity and crush any desire for liberty, instead creating a total dependence on government. Not only are people subsidized, but so are many corporations and the rich too.

How can we resist government's overreach and become a free, empowering and self-governing people once again? For one, we can turn back to God and neighbor. Those who established our form of government believed that we can only preserve our dignity, liberty, and capacity to self-govern if we continue to depend on God. At its inception America based the Big documents (e.g., the Declaration of Independence, the Constitution, and the Bill of Rights) on the idea of a sovereign Creator God who made man in His image and likeness and expects man to treat his fellow man with love, dignity, and respect. They believed that only a moral people focused on following God would be capable of properly governing itself. These, then, are the greatest documents ever written upon which a democratic state can be based and at which it should aim.

The famous and oft quoted second sentence of the Declaration of Independence is the starting point. "We hold these truths to be self-evident that all men are created equal, that they are endowed by **their Creator** with certain unalienable rights, that among these are Life, Liberty and the pursuit of Happiness."

A civil war was fought because 1/8 of the population of this nation was enslaved and not granted these rights. Near the end of that war while dedicating a battlefield in Gettysburg, Va. where many Civil War dead were buried Abraham Lincoln reminded us that" Four score and seven years ago our fathers brought forth on this continent a new nation conceived in liberty and dedicated to the proposition that all men are created equal…" He ended that address stating "…that we here highly resolve that these dead shall not have died in vain – that this nation **under God** shall have a new birth of freedom and that government of the people, by the people and for the people shall not perish from the earth."

The government desires to help, but without the spiritual transformation of the head and heart government cannot develop the social capital of loving thy neighbor. The government's delivery system is incapable on its own of improving this by only laws and money. The government has a vision to empower, but they have no plan or mission to achieve it at the heart level. What we need is a large-scale shift in mindset and heart set from merely thinking about relief to thinking and caring about development, empowerment, self-sufficiency and all in the light of human dignity. The heart transformation is what the Church systems can deliver. It is in mobilizing around our common groan (i.e. the generationally under-resourced child) that our Three Delivery Systems hopefully realize they cannot do this alone, but need each other. If mercy is meant to be temporary, then government subsidies must have a real term limit, decreasing over time while the recipient becomes empowered and self-sufficient. There are any number of possibilities. But after the bleeding stops, the "Iron Rule of Human Development" must apply: "Do not do for those who can do for themselves."

Tragically, in some instances, development is not possible;

earning money is not possible; there is little hope of self-sufficiency. In these cases, the individual must be provided for. But their children and grandchildren have to be justly raised up and empowered to become self-sufficient. In other words, we must develop a unifying vision to mobilize around the poor and blameless child. At the same time, we must not discount the possibility that many families may still be "resourced" when love and justice are relationally applied.

When it comes to working with businesses, churches, and nonprofits, the government's main role will be to make decisions and laws with a bias for the poor, to get the word out and encourage participation in relational programs. But there will also be many opportunities to extend tax breaks and tax credits to businesses that participate in some of the training programs and that eventually provide jobs to the poor and under-employed. More importantly, the government will have to respectfully rein in its tendency to tell nonprofits who they can hire and what they can say. If this program is open to secular nonprofits and to all churches, each faith will have a respectful place at the table. In that way the government is not viewed as "establishing a religion" but rather allowing all an opportunity to participate. This is important, because the heart and soul of touching the poor is the transformational love for God and one's neighbor, which flows out of religious beliefs. Without allowing for this kind of transformation and such free flow of truth and love, the plan to mobilize around the poor child will have little or no success.

Charles Colson used to say that for democratic capitalism to work properly, three things were necessary, each like the leg of a stool. If one did not function properly, the stool tipped over. Those three are economic freedom, political freedom, and moral restraint. (This stool corresponds with our society's three big delivery systems of Business, Government, and Church, each delivering what the others cannot.)

The extent to which we have shifted away from the Founders' view is obvious. Let's take a closer look at the third leg of the stool—moral restraint. For a democracy that is based on capitalism and free enterprise to truly work, the individuals within the democracy need to some extent to adhere to moral principles. That this idea was central to our nation's founding is confirmed by the following statements:

"The religious atmosphere in the country was the first thing that struck me upon my arrival in the U.S. In France, I had seen the spirits of religion and freedom almost always marching in opposite directions. In America, I found them intimately linked together and joined and reigned over the same land…Religion should therefore be considered as the first of their political institutions. From the start politics and religion have agreed and have not since ceased to do so." (Alexis de Tocqueville, *Democracy in America*)

Apparently, many in the business community forgot these truths, and the resulting economic collapse of 2008–09 caused major problems and requiring government bailouts. In his Breakpoint Commentary on May 11, 2009, titled "A Perfect (Cultural) Storm," Chuck Colson clearly described the reasons behind this collapse:

"Today Americans find themselves swept up in the perfect cultural storm. We have a financial meltdown caused largely by moral failures in government, Wall Street, and the public. We're paying the bill for decades of self-indulgence, fueled by rampant relativism, rejection of the Christian work ethic, and materialism."[25]

We know where idolatry leads and it will not be without serious consequences. The root problem is not economic, it is spiritual. As Alexander Solzhenitsyn wrote, describing the decline of another nation:

"More than half a century ago, while I was still a child, I recall hearing a number of older people offer the following explanation for the great disasters that had befallen Russia: "Men have forgotten God; that's why all this happened."

"Since then I have spent well-nigh fifty years working on the history of our Revolution; in the process I have read hundreds of books, collected hundreds of personal testimonies, and have already contributed eight volumes of my own toward the effort of clearing away the rubble left by that upheaval. But if I were asked today to formulate as concisely as possible the main cause of the ruinous Revolution that swallowed up some sixty million of our people, I could not put it more accurately than to repeat: "Men have forgotten God; that's why all this has happened."[26]

In the business community a different mindset and heartset has to develop. Businessmen can earn a profit while still being good stewards.

Working to tackle the individual and social causes of

---

[25] Chuck Colson, "A Perfect (Cultural) Storm," *The Christian Post,* May 13, 2009, https://www.christianpost.com/Opinion/Columns/2009/05/a-perfect-cultural-storm-13/.

[26] Aleksandr Solzhenitsyn, "Templeton Lecture: London, Guildhall, May 10, 1983," in *The Solzhenitsyn Reader: New and Essential Writings 1947–2005,* ed. Edward E. Ericson, Jr. and Daniel J. Mahoney (Wilmington, DE: ISI Books, 2006), 577.

generational poverty will require heart transformation, mutually beneficial relationships, education, life skills, job training, and jobs. Looking again at the Baton Rouge Advocate of March 15, 2009:

"Many people are one big expense away from being on the street," said Catholic Charities spokeswoman Carol Spruell. "If their car breaks down, what's the likelihood of them having $1000 in the bank in order to get the car repaired?" Spruell said. "A lot of people are one illness away from homelessness. It's a huge hurdle to overcome" …

Another necessary aspect is the involvement of coworkers in the training process. Two important needs of any individual are the desire for love and the desire for significance. What greater significance is there in a job than to know you are helping a person find a new direction in their life? According to a recent newspaper article by Jeannine Aversa, the AP economics reporter, job satisfaction in America is at a twenty-two-year low.[27] She writes, "…only 45% of Americans are satisfied with their work. That was the lowest level ever recorded by the Conference board research group in more than 22 years of studying the issue. In 2008, 49% of those surveyed reported satisfaction with their jobs." She goes on to say that this dissatisfaction has been on the rise for two decades and, if not reversed, "could stifle innovation and hurt America's competitiveness and productivity. And it could make unhappy older workers less inclined to take the time to share their

---

[27] Anita Kissee & Jeannine Aversa, "Americans' job satisfaction falls to record low," January 4, 2010, https://kval.com/news/local/americans-job-satisfaction-falls-to-record-low.

knowledge and skills with younger workers." While some of the obvious problems include income not keeping up with inflation and rising health costs, a big factor is that "fewer workers consider their jobs to be interesting." While not all jobs can be interesting, they can still have significance if the proper goals are kept in mind. One such goal is the sharing of job knowledge and skills with fellow employees. What could be more significant to a dissatisfied employee than knowing he or she is cared for, heard and would make a real difference in someone's life? In understanding that our work is a sacred gift from God, it becomes a higher calling and source of meaning and purpose.

Any concrete plan will require much more detail, but these ideas are a good starting place for those church, government, and business systems that have a deep desire for wholeness and peace – systems that will mobilize their mutually beneficial networks and resources around their common groan, the blameless and generationally under-resourced child.

Conclusion

The question remains: Can we bring an end to generational poverty?

Yes, we are promised this if we courageously follow Jesus' Agape Way given to us in His all-encompassing Greatest Commandments. God's edifying human resources will flow to all in these right and caring relationships. And although it has been stated multiple times in this book, one of the most important issues we each have to deal with is "idols" that break these right and caring relationships and limit God's empowering resource flows.

If we still believe we do not have any idols then we need to truly consider those things which we love the most and that unknowingly control and direct our lives. We are all affected by America's Holy Trinity: Individualism; Materialism; and Ethnocentrism. At least one or more of these likely play a controlling part in our lives and the lives of others. We are told to "first take the log from *our* own eye, then *we* will see well enough to deal with the speck in *our* friend's eye" (Matthew 7:5 NLT). That is, in recognizing and dealing with our individual and cultural idols we will be in a better position to love God and our neighbor rightly. When we begin seeing those who are under-resourced as our neighbor, get face to face with them as friends (relocate), confess to God that we have not properly cared (reconcile), commit to Jesus' Greatest Commandments, then our idols begin to dissolve. In the unifying process of developing transformational habits that reflect the character of Jesus (individually and collectively) we become well-equipped by God's grace and begin the process of ending generational poverty (redeem). We use the phrase "begin the process" because all development takes time… and requires us to honor God's process.

We have to first realize and believe that each of us is experiencing poverty in at least one of the 6 major dimensions of human wellness and development: socially, economically, educationally, emotionally, physically and in all spiritually. First, this will remove any idea that we are saviors but rather fellow sojourners. In the process we become less prideful and more humble (Phil 2:3) and thus more willing to contribute to the "bank" of social capital (i.e., loving our neighbor) in our communities. In addition to understanding these needed human resources, poverty alleviation (without causing harm) will also require an understanding of the dignity of man, the indignity of poverty from one generation to another, poverty's many dimensions, the root causes of poverty, God's solution to poverty, strengthening of social capital, and mobilizing relational networks from our community's 3-Delivery Systems (Church, Business and Government) around the blameless, generationally poor child. In right and caring relationships community resources will begin to flow down like a river on our generationally poor, vulnerable and blameless child.

Just take a look at Bridge Ministry of Acadiana. BMA is a working example of trying to resource our under-resourced neighbors and neighborhood without causing further harm. BMA is a Christian Community Development Organization that follows the principles of "development" espoused in this book. In learning how to love our neighbors BMA discovered a common groan in our neighborhood and in our community for the generationally under-resourced child. As such BMA is currently building further social capital networks (i.e., friendships) around the children at Holy Family Catholic School (HFCS) that Love, Educate, & Transform. HFCS is a high poverty (92% Qualify for Free & Reduced Lunches) school that is in BMA's neighborhood. We want the best for all our children. BMA's goal is to further mobilize our community's social, economic, educational, emotional, physical and spiritual resources and networks around our economically poor children. In building relational networks that develop and empower, BMA has joined our community's Catholic Networks by partnering with HFCS. HFCS is under Bishop Deshotel, the Diocese of Lafayette, three church Parishes, and the Catholic Church Community. In this partnership BMA serves under our principal, Mr. Griffin, to serve the HFCS students and their parents by extending their school day and extending their school year in the summer. And, BMA being an all denominational ministry invites all churches to join us in loving our neighbors. BMA's immediate goal is to close our under-resourced children's Achievement Gap. BMA provides 3 hours of after school programs that include 1 hour of tutoring led by professional teachers and mentors. BMA serves snacks and a hot meal daily. There are also Life Skills, Soft Skills and Character building activities for 1.5 hours per day too. Our Summer Programs are composed of these same elements from 7:30 to 3:30. Our classes have no more that 10 children per Teacher and Mentor (5:1 student/adult ratio). In serving HFCS, Bridge has many volunteering opportunities to join through reading to children, doing math, teaching social and workplace etiquette, dance, music, and art. Outside the HFCS partnership BMA also has neighborhood development opportunities, neighborhood bible studies, administration and IT jobs, Campus maintenance like plumbing, painting, carpentry, pressure washing, gardening, Volunteer Development & Coordinating opportunities, become a Church Ambassador for BMA. Take a class on a swamp tour, fishing trips, any field trips that broaden our children's horizons is critical. Can you cook? Come cook for our parent-teachers' nights. Do you like sports? Come lead and teach our children a sport... or even chess or hobby.... Over the years we have offered a variety of opportunities to those individuals and church groups who desire the opportunity to meet, learn and love their neighbor. We have picked up litter in the neighborhood; prayer walks, cut trees; built vegetable gardens; rebuilt neighbor's porches; refloored some of their homes; worked on roofs; and on one occasion completely remodeled a house.

BMA is simply a vehicle where our churches, businesses and even government can come together, meet and begin learning to love their neighbor as we learn to love ourselves… BMA is a vehicle that relationally resources our under-resourced neighbors along the pathway of love…. advantaging the disadvantaged. Our motto is "Love, Educate and Transform". Come become a Team player.

You can partner with a Bridge Ministry type entity or any non-profit in your area by Volunteering, Investing and/or Praying. **Just look around your area to see where God is working and go there!**

Our common groan is why the authors say that the generationally poor child holds the key to our wholeness, individually and collectively. Yes, we can end poverty…. God promises us that if we follow His Way, our idols will die and there should be no poor among us (Deut 15:4-5).

Jesus said, "Let the little children come to me, and do not hinder them, for the kingdom of heaven belongs to such as these." (Matthew 19:14, NIV)

The generationally under-resourced & blameless child holds the key to our wholeness, individually and collectively.

K2 SERIES
CONTACT INFORMATION
Email address: **K2@k2series.com**
Website: www.K2series.com
Follow us on Facebook: K2series
Purchase the *K2 SERIES* books: on Amazon
Amazon reviews are appreciated.

Made in the USA
Monee, IL
30 August 2021